D0277053

WATCHDOG

THE CONSUMER SURVIVAL GUIDE

WATCHDOG

THE CONSUMER SURVIVAL GUIDE

MATT ALLWRIGHT

BBC BOOKS

I

BBC Books, an imprint of Ebury Publishing
20 Vauxhall Bridge Road,
London SW I V 2SA

BBC Books is part of the Penguin Random House group
of companies whose addresses can be found at global.
penguinrandomhouse.com

Penguin
Random House
UK

This book is published to accompany the BBC's
Watchdog first broadcast in 1980

First published by BBC Books in 2020

www.penguin.co.uk

A CIP catalogue record for this book is available from
the British Library

ISBN 9781785945359

Design by seagulls.net

Contents

Introduction

Hello! Matt here! Welcome to Watchdog: The Consumer Survival Guide! I heartily recommend you carry this with you at all times, wherever you go, either in a sturdy, re-useable bag or in your head. I also recommend you read it in the following manner, depending on how much time you've got:

1 If you've got five minutes, just read p. 6. There are a few rules to live by which just might stick in your noggin and save you money/dignity/happiness.

2 Fifteen or twenty minutes? Read that first page and then the chapter on the law and your rights, starting on p. 8. This will also equip you for shop arguments and dinner parties, especially if the wine you bought isn't that good and needs to go back.

3 If time is on your side, read those bits and then everything else, in whichever order you choose, whenever you fancy. Read it upside down if you like. It's your book now. You're the boss.

Why did I write it? Well, no-one can know everything about everything. Particularly when it comes to our money and how we spend it, there are just too many subjects, and those subjects are then divided into a bewildering plethora of A-roads, then B-road sub-topics. To be master or mistress of each and every one of them is impossible. There are certainly too many to fit into just one book. This means that eventually, when you're handing over money, you have to trust someone to know more than you do. Whether it's because you're asking them to prune your acacia or sell you a mortgage, you're relying on someone to say, 'This is what I do. I know what you need and, for a reasonable price, I know how to give it to you. Trust me.' And trust them you will. Yes, there are laws to protect us, but at the end of the day it's going to come down to the trust between two people. There simply isn't time in the day to investigate every company and every transaction we make. It would, quite frankly, be exhausting.

> You're relying on someone to say, 'This is what I do. I know what you need and, for a reasonable price, I know how to give it to you. Trust me.'

But just because you can't possibly know everything about everything, that doesn't mean you can't work out a few simple rules to live by to steer you away from those who you can't trust and towards the good guys. Over 23 years on *Watchdog* and *Rogue Traders*, talking to people who've been unlucky and occasionally unwise, a few big, simple themes have started to emerge for me, and that's what I've tried to give you here. I can't say I'm an expert in any of the subjects we cover in this book. Oh, the experts are out there! If you fancy digging around on the internet, in papers and in magazines, you will go down a dizzying rabbit hole of specialist knowledge, but that's not our purpose here. You can easily spend a week finding out all about domestic pipe sizing – metric and imperial. But I think that sometimes you need to start from first principles, to imagine that no-one knows anything, and then try to navigate over the big hurdles and around the gaping elephant traps that face us all. That's what I'm trying to do: create a survival guide that reminds us how things work and why they sometimes don't, and point out the ways in which people who don't deserve your money often go about getting it. Once you've spotted the Big Idea behind each devious scheme and scam, there's a good chance you're equipped for a few more down the road.

Added to this I'm going to try to wedge in lots of real-life examples and experiences from the programmes that I've now been involved with for the best part of my adult life. All of these are stories we've worked up and investigated over the last three decades of fighting the good fight. It's important to see practical examples of when things go wrong, and take a lasting lesson from each one. TV is, on the whole, not an enduring medium, and it's always a bit disappointing when a great story has had its hour in the sun and then fizzles out. Putting these stories in book form means that their power to help people is given its second legs and a life outside of their flickering hour on the box.

It's the least my fantastic colleagues deserve. *Watchdog* and my baby, *Rogue Traders*, are unlike any other environments I've ever worked in. To put it simply, we all believe. From my first week in the office I realised how seriously the teams took the job we'd been given. I also learned that television doesn't have to be a cynical illusion: the organisation you see on the screen, trying to help and protect people throughout their lives, may indeed be a group of talented and committed journalists, film-makers, producers and researchers who think that what they're doing is the right thing to do. We have always taken time to argue and debate about the moral issues behind your tumble drier, your roof and your broadband, knowing that while they may not be seen as weighty next to matters political and newsy, they make up much bigger parts of our lives, and they matter massively to us all. Long before *Gogglebox* we envisioned ourselves sitting on the sofa at home next to you, trying to imagine what you'd say about the stories we'd cover. Over the years, occasionally there would be a focus group or two, but in most cases

> *We have always taken time to argue and debate about the moral issues behind your tumble drier, your roof and your broadband.*

we have relied on our gut and our own experiences and conversations to tell us what matters most, and for the most part (apart from the one item I did about high-end fountain pens) I think we got it right.

People often ask me if I enjoy my job. In most cases I think they already know the answer. I love what I do. It's as close as I can imagine the real world offers to being in a Spaghetti Western. I ride into town and get the chance to put things straight and give people an answer. People come to us because they feel let down and exploited and they don't feel they have anyone to turn to. For the most part they realise that their money has gone, but with the best stories, it's not really about the money. From my experience what they're really after is to know that there's someone there who will listen, who won't, in the words of Vic and Bob, let it lie, and who is, unequivocally, on their side. I'd really like this book to be a lasting part of the *Watchdog* idea that's been going for all these years, and more than anything, I hope you find it genuinely useful.

People come to us because they feel let down and exploited and they don't feel they have anyone to turn to.

Pass it on!

Lots of love,
            Matt

Watchdog
in Brief

People lead busy lives. Let's say you haven't got time to read this whole thing – here's a rundown of the essentials you'll come across as you go through. If you take nothing else away, stitch these useful little ideas into the lining of your coat.

→ **SQUAD Fit For Life.** The Consumer Rights Act 2015 means that goods you buy must be **s**atisfactory in **qu**ality and **as** **d**escribed. (Take the first letters of the words and think of this as **SQUAD**.) Goods must be **f**it **for** purpose and have a reasonable **l**ife span. (Remember, **fit for life.**) Put that together and what have you got? **Squad, fit for life.**

← **OOTBNFY.** **O**ut **o**f **T**he **B**lue? **N**ot **f**or **Y**ou. Don't trust any offer that comes from an outside source, unsolicited.

➜ **Feels unfair? You know where**! If a deal feels sneaky, take a peeky at the Consumer Protection from Unfair Trading Regulations 2008. There's a good chance what just stung you is outlined and outlawed in there.

← **Plastic is fantastic!** Section 75 of the Consumer Credit Act says that if you buy anything over £100 on your credit card, the card provider is jointly liable if anything goes wrong. Don't have one? Get one! But pay it off every month.

➜ **Be Marvellous Marvin Haggler**. Don't hand over money without jabbing away at the price and other elements of the deal. You'll be surprised what you can achieve when you haggle. And silence is golden. If in doubt, sit, wait and watch the price drop.

← **SDCD. Snap decision, cr*p decision**. If you're being forced to do a deal in a restricted time frame, that's a deal you don't want.

➜ **ERASER**. When the time comes to complain, be **E**mpathetic, **R**easonable, **A**ssertive, **S**upported, **E**videnced and **R**elentless, and watch your complaint disappear!

Short but sweet. Now, you've got a bus to catch! Places to go! People to see!

chapter
one

Meet Your New Legal Team

The law is on your side. It might not feel like it when you're standing at a checkout with a shrunken t-shirt, or arguing online about a phone charger that won't charge, but at your shoulder, waiting its turn, is a team of superhero bits of legislation ready to swing into action and – KERPOW! – fight alongside you to ensure that common sense and justice win the day.

There are a few legendary laws you should have on speed dial, and then a few very handy specialist sidekicks who can come in to save the day when the Big Guns appear to be tied to the train tracks. I've placed these in the order of how potent or frequently used I reckon they are, but a word of warning: By the time you've read this section, you will know more about consumer law than 95 per cent of the people you are dealing with out there in the world of pounds and pence. Be gentle but firm with them, and remember, these are your rights in law, and quite different from company or shop policy, which can only add to them, but never take away. In any argument, they are non-negotiable: the ace in the hole, and the knockout punch.

> By the time you've read this section, you will know more about consumer law than 95 per cent of the people you are dealing with.

Consumer Rights Act 2015: Doctor Sort-it

This one knows how to get things done! Like a certain legendary time-travelling Doctor, the CRA 2015 is a regeneration of decades-old bits of law brought together in one deceptively spacious police box. If you don't commit any other law to memory, take this one down. Well, not all 11 chapters, 101 sections and additional 10 schedules. Just take the important bits, which hopefully I've made a bit more straightforward here.

Write it on a bit of paper and stick it in your wallet if you must, but don't leave home without it.

WHAT DOES IT DO?

It's there to make sure that whatever you're promised, in terms of goods or services, you get it, not just at the point when you buy it, but for a REASONABLE period afterwards. Squad! SQUAD attention!

Goods must be of a:

Satisfactory
QUality,
As
Described

So that's the first bit. The next bit is that our superhero law insists that they have to do their job well, and keep on doing it. To do that they must be **fit** for purpose and have a REASONABLE **lifeE**span:

Fit For Life

So there we have it. **SQUAD Fit For Life**. An easy way to remember the single most important cover-all consumer law there is, and, while we're at it, a terrific marketing slogan for a personal trainer. So that pretty much wraps it up.

What's that? Eh?

Ah yes. You'll have noticed that, despite me putting in capitals, at no point has anyone explained what the crucial word REASONABLE means. And one person's reasonable is another person's completely unacceptable. You don't want to be arguing semantics at the till with a queue behind you. One of the great things they did in 2015 was to put a bit more chocolate on the Wagon Wheel of what 'reasonable' actually means, which is handy if you're unfortunate enough to have to put it to the test in front of a car dealer or somewhat begrudging weekend worker in a sports warehouse.

30 DAYS

If the thing you've bought isn't SQUAD Fit and you return it within 30 days from the moment you bought it, you are entitled to a full refund. Isn't that beautifully simple? Let's leave it there then.

OK, it's not that simple. Obviously if you buy a pint of semi-skimmed from a supermarket and try to return it as unfit for purpose 29 days later, they will laugh in your face. You're clearly trying to milk it. Perishable goods are only protected up to their use-by date. Also digital downloads and services don't automatically get a full refund if they develop a fault. You should still ask for them to be repaired or replaced, or get a partial refund. Everything else? 30 days!

AFTER 30 DAYS

Aha! No automatic refund now for you, buddy, but whoever sold you the darn thing gets one go to put it right – that's either by repairing or replacing. You can say which you'd rather, but in the end, it's up to them which one they provide. In certain circumstances, you can insist on a full or partial refund, usually when repairing or replacing is impractical for you, for instance, if the thing has to go away for a year to be repaired and you don't get to use it during that time, or if a repair is impractical or impossible to get it back to what you were promised in the first place. Then you're within your legal rights to say, 'Oi, mush, don't bother, just give me my money back', although this accent only really works if you're buying something from the market in *EastEnders*.

If, after that first go, the thing still doesn't match up to SQUAD Fit For Life goals, you can insist on that refund that's been waiting in the wings, or if you like, and you're a glutton for punishment, give them another chance to put it right. This **can't** be used by them as a way to run down the clock though. The crucial time period is between taking possession of the item and making the complaint. Until it's resolved, the space–time continuum is frozen – at least until…

THE FIRST SIX MONTHS

This is why I love this version of this law. It's so Jodie Whittaker kickass. Spot something that's not SQUAD Fit compliant within the half-year and the law assumes that's the way it was when you bought it. It's up to the retailer to prove it wasn't. How cool is that? Cars are a bit different. After 30 days dealers are within their rights to deduct the value of whatever use you got from the motor.

AFTER THAT…

… until the end of time … the burden of proof flips to you to show you didn't cause whatever it was that made your purchase not SQUAD Fit compliant. It doesn't mean the fight's over, and you can still go for the refund/replace one-time option if you can show there was a pre-existing fault or defect. But don't go back to TK Maxx with a five-year-old pair of shoes you've worn every day, complain that they've lost their shine and expect to receive a warm and sympathetic welcome. That's all I'm saying. REASONABLE is still the

> *Don't go back to TK Maxx with a five-year-old pair of shoes you've worn every day, complain that they've lost their shine and expect to receive a warm and sympathetic welcome.*

> *Most retailers give little or no emphasis to consumer rights in staff training, and that means you may have to do a bit of rapid till-side education at some point in your life.*

key here, even if the Good Doctor CRA 2015 has inked in a bit more of the detail for everyone.

JUDGE MATT'S VERDICT

OK, SQUAD, now you know the CRA 2015. I can pretty much guarantee you that the next retail assistant you come across when you need to use it won't have a clue that it exists. Most retailers give little or no emphasis to consumer rights in staff training, and that means you may have to do a bit of rapid till-side education at some point in your life. The most common confusion for retail employees is between your rights under law and the shop's policy. While the law can't be sidestepped or changed, policy may vary from one retailer to another, and can be abandoned entirely for sale or damaged items. It's worth checking out store policy before buying, and adding it to your now supercharged consumer knowledge. It's also worth remembering that it isn't the fault of an individual employee if they haven't been trained up in the most fundamental element of their jobs. As always, keep your cool and stick to your guns. The law is your silver bullet every time.

The Consumer Protection from Unfair Trading Regulations 2008: The Rogue Buster

Catchy, huh? Yep, that's why I like to call it 'The Rogue Traders Bible'. If we're continuing the superhero theme here, this amazing Swiss Army Knife of a law is standing, pants outside tights, with a packed utility belt full of amazing gizmos to combat dodgepots. It's particularly good at weeding out those who would sell you things in a dishonest or unscrupulous manner.

Words can't express how marvellous I think this law is. It's a good way to show you if you're dealing with a bunch of bandits, then let them know that you know they're up to no good, and spread the word around. It's even more useful for enforcement agencies like Trading Standards to be able to issue fines and sanctions. But it's become more useful for us as consumers since 2014, as you can now also use a breach of the 2008 CPFUTR as a basis to cancel a contract and get a refund.

> This amazing Swiss Army Knife of a law is standing, pants outside tights, with a packed utility belt full of amazing gizmos to combat dodgepots.

WHAT DOES IT DO?

The reason this law is so wonderful is that it first gives a general description of what is 'unfair' and 'dishonest': in essence, anything that misleads, causing the target to make a purchase or 'transactional decision' they wouldn't have otherwise. This can be because of something that's been said during the sales process, but equally something that was left out (for example, this car has no wheels). It also requires traders to stick to any industry body guidelines to which they've signed up, giving those guidelines a legal edge.

But then, rather magnificently, it also goes on to outline a whole list of specific practices that are just outright against the law. Thirty-one of the beauties. I won't go into all of them, but if you read the pressure selling section in the Scam chapter (p. 28), then you'll see why it's so useful in those transactions. For instance, you're an outlaw if you:

➡ Say that an offer is time limited when it isn't.

⬅ Stay when you've been asked to leave, or come back or ring when you've been told not to.

➡ Say that something is a free service when it isn't.

⬅ Start to sell a person one thing, then change to the thing you were really trying to flog (bait and switch).

➡ Claim to be part of, or use the badges of, an industry body or federation when you're not.

Matt Nav

The first company to be convicted of offences under the 2008 CPFUT regs was… (drum roll)… a double glazing company! Quelle surprise! Show some originality at least, Safestyle (UK)! Back in 2011 they were had up because they didn't leave poor John Wigmore of Bottesford, Lincolnshire, alone, contacting him at least a dozen times despite him asking them not to. They ended up paying £22,000 in fines and legal costs. Double glazing: good for protecting you from the cold, not so good for keeping cold calling away.

What this shows is that it doesn't take large numbers of complaints to make the CPFUT regs work. If it's unfair, it's illegal, and it only needs one case to make it stick.

Matt Stat

Bad business doesn't just affect the customer. The Ombudsman Services Report (2017) reckons that poor customer service costs businesses £37 billion a year. Get it right – everyone's a winner!'

← Make false claims about the purchaser being at risk if they don't buy.

→ Say that your job will be at risk if you don't make the sale.

And quite a few more. Combining a general idea that you can't mislead people to make a sale with specific practices that are instantly unlawful makes for a real belt-and-braces approach that we've been able to use on the programme a load of times. Once you start looking through the banned practices, it's really common sense that they shouldn't be allowed. Bravo, lawmakers!

Consumer Contracts Regulations: Your online fortnightly friend

Well now, what have we here? A law that protects me when I'm not even making a purchase face to face, you say? How intriguing! Until 2014 these purchases were pretty much covered by the Distance Selling Regulations – more descriptive, but less comprehensive.

With the massive growth of online selling, this law is now bang up to date. The most important bit is your right, in law, to cancel any contract that's not made on shop premises, face to face. This is often called a 'cooling off period'. Obviously this is massively useful for online sales, but applies equally when you're being sold to in your own home, or elsewhere. It also lays down some common sense basics. Some of the things you must be told:

→ What you're buying. An accurate description, including any lasting contractual commitment, monthly payments, etc.

← How and when you're going to pay.

→ Exactly who it is that's selling it to you.

← Delivery charges: how much and who's paying them.

→ Cost and method of returning things if they're not right.

← Your rights to cancel.

And that last one is key. Now we come to the rule of fortnights. Typically, you'll have **14 days** to cancel, although in practice this is a stretchy fortnight. The 14 days start from when you receive your goods – but you can cancel from the moment you place your order. If there's a delay between the two, as there usually is, that's added to your cooling off period. After that you've got another 14 days to send the goods back, and you should get a refund a further 14 days after that. Neat, huh? Services are different, by the way. The cooling off period starts when you sign (or click) the contract. This is not great because it means that the provider can then deliver the service on day 15, giving you no make-your-mind-up time.

WHAT DOESN'T IT COVER?

There are some exclusions to the CCR 2014. Some of these make sense, and others are a bit nicky-nacky-noo and open to abuse. Digital media, CDs and DVDs aren't covered. Neither are perishable goods. The items have to go back in the same condition they arrived, or you can be docked the difference from your refund, so take pictures as you're shipping.

The real kicker, though, is that if your item is bespoke or made-to-measure – that is, manufactured to your specifications – the cooling off period doesn't apply. From a practical point of view this makes sense: if the manufacturer starts making something to fit you, they will struggle to find someone else to buy it if it's returned. However, I've seen too many rogue furniture salesmen use this as a way to sell off-the-peg chairs and beds made overseas without the risk of customers having second thoughts and cancelling.

The Consumer Credit Act 2006: The Loan Ranger

Sometimes we need to get stuff on credit. It's a painful necessity of life that we might have to pay a bit of interest when we do. But here's a wonderful thing: because of this epic bit of legislation, getting stuff on credit can actually IMPROVE your situation if things go wrong. Yippee ki-yay! Sorry.

WHAT IT DOES

This act tries to impose a bit of law and order on the Wild West that used to be consumer credit. It says that if you're taking out credit, whether it's in the form of a loan, a hire purchase agreement or spending on your credit card, you need to know what you're letting yourself in for, who you're dealing with, and that you can get out if you need to. It also grants you some protections which are incredibly useful, and acts as a deterrent by telling companies they will be run out of town and lose their right to legally offer credit if they don't play nice. In short:

- You must be given accurate, clear information about the agreement.

- You must know exactly who is providing the credit, and any intermediaries involved.

- You must know the amount, schedule and term of the repayments.

- You must be told the interest payable, expressed as Annual Percentage Rate (APR).

- You have to be given this information before you're given the actual agreement to sign.

- Whoever's giving you credit has to make sure you can afford it – usually by using a credit rating service.

Credit agreements come with their own cooling off periods – that's separate and in addition to the ones outlined above in the CCR 2014. This starts with a five-day period where you can cancel the credit with no charges whatsoever. It's like the thing never existed. After that we're into the world of fortnights again. You've got 14 days after that when you can cancel, but you will be liable for any interest that's accrued during that time. But here comes arguably the most important part of the CCA 2006:

Section 75

This might be the single most useful bit of consumer law ever written. It's certainly the bit of advice I give, and hear given by others the most. It protects when all else fails, provides a backstop against losing out that trumps all others and is a friend in need when you're up against it, like having Daley Thompson step out of the gents loos to settle an argument in a pub.

WHAT IT DOES

Section 75 of the CCA 2006 says that if you buy something worth between £100 and £30,000 on a credit card, then the credit card provider is jointly liable with whoever you're buying from for the thing or service that's bought. In practice, let's say you spend £5,000 on a family holiday, but before you get to travel, the holiday company goes bust. You have no insurance, and the company is not protected by ATOL or any other industry body. In the absence of any other recourse, the credit card company must reimburse you for your losses. How amazing is that?

If the company goes out of business, that's pretty clear cut, but if the good or service doesn't come up to scratch in some way or breaches its contract and you can't get the firm to sort it out, then the card company has to do it. You don't even have to wait until the good or service provider stops helping. You can apply to the card company at the same time. Tell them I sent you, and that you know exactly what you're doing.

> *In the absence of any other recourse, the credit card company must reimburse you for your losses.*

Another time to whip out the credit card for a payment is when you're dealing with companies overseas – when you know that simply rocking up and knocking on a door isn't going to be easy – or when you're shopping online and the seller's identity isn't immediately apparent. A word of warning though: if you use a payment system like Paypal, backed up with your credit card as the source of funds, Section 75 doesn't apply. It has to be a direct payment.

To be clear: I'm not encouraging you to start racking up huge debt on your credit card. Interest rates can be

> *A word of warning though: if you use a payment system like Paypal, backed up with your credit card as the source of funds, Section 75 doesn't apply.*

painful and can quickly get out of control. But if you pay off your card bill every month, avoiding any interest, I'd say it's worth having a credit card in your wallet just for the protection you get from Section 75. You only have to make a couple of big purchases before you'll start noticing a curious peaceful state of mind emerging. You will start to whistle, pat small children on the head and smile at traffic wardens.

'Section 75?' they will ask, and you will nod wisely.

Here are a couple of other bits of law that you might need, hopefully less often:

General Data Protection Regulations: The Data General

Stand up straight, firms! This came in in 2018 and tells companies they can't mess around with your data.

➡ They can't share it with anyone you don't want to see it.

⬅ They can only process it if they've got a good reason (there are six clearly outlined).

→ You have to give explicit permission if it is to be used for others' marketing purposes – it can't be something from which you have to opt OUT. If it's to be used by the company with whom you directly have a contract, you have to have the right to opt out at any time.

← You can see the data held about you within a month of filing a Subject Access Request – and you can have it corrected if it's wrong.

→ If your data leaks out, you have to be told as soon as possible, and you should be compensated for any loss incurred.

A quick note on COVID-19 here. As I'm writing there are many, many areas of our consumer life which are being affected by the global pandemic. We're seeing a lot of firms using this as a reason, and certainly, sometimes as an excuse, for denying us our rights as laid out over the last couple of pages. It's very simple. They can't. If they don't like the laws here, or if enforcing them puts them at the risk of going bust, that's a matter for them to take up with the government who makes the laws. It's not a reason to say you can't have a refund, or get your goods as described, or change your mind within 14 days. So, don't accept it, and don't forget company policy NEVER trumps your consumer rights in law, it can only add to it.

It *is*, however, worth considering what will happen if you do insist on your rights when firms are so hard pushed.

Matt Nav

The GDPR regs are backed up with huge maximum fines – 10 million euros or 4 per cent of annual global turnover, whichever is higher – so companies take them really seriously. However, on *Watchdog* we still report fairly regularly on data breaches from some of the biggest names around. British Airways was fined a whopping £183 million for letting customer data slip through the net, and Marriott Hotels took a hit of nearly £100 million. But if you think of the damage that can be done by giving dodgepots access to millions of customer records, then it feels about right. We trust these companies to keep our details away from identity thieves and fraudsters. If their systems aren't up to it, a light slap on the wrist isn't going to make them change their ways. GDPR caused a right rumpus when it was introduced, with firms having to get up to speed very quickly. If the massive penalties hadn't been there, a few may have dragged their feet.

If the company concerned does go bust, you might lose your money anyway. Think about ways you could still get what you want, which also makes life easier for the company, for instance, a better holiday later on. Use the ERASER complaining formula, and a little bit of light Marvin Haggling!

chapter
two

Scams

One of the most heartbreaking
parts of my job is talking to people
who have been the target of a scam.
The effects can be devastating: not
just waving a permanent farewell
to thousands of pounds, but also –
much more damaging – often saying
goodbye to big chunks of self-esteem
and trust in the people around you.

Scams ruin lives, and yet they rarely get investigated or prosecuted, despite us losing an estimated £7 billion to fraudsters every year. But even that's a tip-of-the-iceberg figure if I ever saw one. The National Crime Agency, who published that number, reckons less than 20 per cent of frauds get reported. Less than 1 per cent of police officers work in specialist fraud teams, despite the fact fraud makes up 31 per cent of all crime. One final stat for you: only 3 per cent of fraud investigations lead to criminal charges.

The point I'm making here is that there's a lot of it about. I've seen it do terrible damage and you can't rely on anyone else to either protect you or sort it out afterwards.

Scams ruin lives, and yet they rarely get investigated or prosecuted, despite us losing an estimated £7 billion to fraudsters every year.

THE BASICS

Depressed by that intro? Don't be! You have this book in your hands right now, and that means you are in the perfect position to protect yourself and others against fraud before it gets messy! The other great news is that most frauds follow just a few basic models. However, just like manufacturers of crisps, scammers will give them a slightly different flavour every year to make you think you're getting something new. Once you've spotted the basic themes, you're wise for life, because crisps, at the end of the day, will always be crisps.

The other thing we should get out of our heads straight away is that scams are only for other people. Call them what you want – gullible, naive, foolish, greedy – but the truth is we can all be the victim of a scam. We all want things, whether it's to get our computer fixed, find a job or life partner, make a profitable investment or get a bit of loft insulation, and scams are there to appear to offer these things and many, many others without ever coming good on the deal. Everyone's got a scam trigger – an area where we're prepared to put logic and method to one side for a bit to get what we want or need. If yours hasn't found you yet then I'm glad. I've certainly been scammed in the past. I don't want it to happen to you.

The nuts and bolts of each scam are often starkly apparent after it has played out. Scammers cast around trying to find your trigger – and that might include feelings of fear, desire, greed, loneliness or obligation. The most unscrupulous will peg their scam on a major international disaster (COVID-19, anyone?), while solar power, boiler replacements, digital aerials and other topical talking points have all become vehicles for villains. Before you know it, you are doing something that, in the cold light of day, you never would.

> *Everyone's got a scam trigger.*

Before we start: a phrase to carry in your top pocket with you wherever you go. Most authorities who give advice on scams use the following words to help people sort sheep from goats, wheat from chaff etc.: 'If it seems too good to be true, it probably is.'

You will see it written an AWFUL lot. I have to confess I have a problem with the logic of this. Most of us are looking for opportunities that others seem to have missed. It's the way of the free market world. If we followed this advice, would we ever buy anything? After all, by definition, making a purchase requires us to think that on some level, we are getting a better deal than the person selling the thing. Also, 'too good to be true' is the sort of thing that people only work out AFTER they've been scammed, not before. So many scams are totally believable until the moment your money is gone. But if that phrase is a tad overused and redundant, how else can we protect ourselves?

Well, after spending years in a laboratory working intensively with combinations of words, I have manufactured this additional phrase which I'm pretty sure will kill 70 per cent of all known scams DEAD. OK, not as good as a certain brand of bleach, but still, not bad eh? What's more, it works BEFORE the money's been flushed away:

OUT OF THE BLUE? NOT FOR YOU! (OOTBNFY)

To explain: any opportunity that comes unsolicited, without request or initiation, is not an opportunity in which you, as someone I care about, should be interested. It doesn't matter if it's in the form of a Facebook advert, an email, a phone call, a conversation with a friend, a fax or carried by a woodland creature in a tiny leather bag, if it's not a contact **you've** made after carefully researching the thing you want, then you don't want the thing that you are being offered. Right! You are equipped with your scam-proof coat and hat! Let's start working our way through a few of the many flavours of scam available before I get sued by Gary Lineker or Domestos.

INVESTMENT SCAMS

This is a classic flavour-of-the-month scam, where the currency of the tabloid press is harnessed to rip you off.

Seen a headline about the growth of the carbon offsetting industry? Guess what! Here's an out-of-the-blue call about investing in carbon credits. Change in the pension law to allow people early access to their pots? Here's a nice man on the phone who knows how to get a rate of interest on that money that a savings account or annuity could never match! Ooh, look! Here's a lovely feature in the Sunday papers about how wine or whisky increases in value over time. And what's this? An email which quotes that feature and invites me to be a part of this wonderful way to cash in on my hobby. Expect initial investments to be low, as a way of building trust. You may even see returns on those investments – on paper at least – to give a spur to further outlay. Then, when the harbinger with the headset is no longer a stranger, but a friend, expect to have to make a quick decision on spending more than you're comfortable with on something that is a stone-cold certainty to turn a profit. And then prepare yourself for the long, quiet evenings waiting for that person to call back.

Matt Nav

Boiler rooms are short-term let offices full of young people wearing headsets who probably don't know how much damage they're doing. They are usually run by slightly older people who know exactly what they're doing, and don't care. The young people are usually working from a script, convincing people to part with money for things which they will never receive, or which will never happen, but because of the nature of these scams, they aren't totally aware of what happens at the end of the process they're initiating. They could probably work it out if they thought about it, but they are generally young people who have struggled to find work, and suddenly they have been given a job that pays commission according to their success, as well as a boss who looks like the success they want, and encourages and incentivises them every step of the way. If you want an idea of this, watch *The Wolf of Wall Street*, or *Glengarry Glen Ross*. I know this because I've walked into a few of these rooms and had to bring these young people up to speed on the reality of what they're doing, sometimes using a megaphone so that they can all hear me. It's never easy and they're never pleased to see me. I end up thinking that in their own way, they are also victims of the scam. I never think that about their boss.

ADVANCE FEE FRAUD

This is where it gets nasty, international and just a little bit scary. Out Of The Blue (You see? It WORKS!) you receive an email (it used to be a fax) saying that if you help with a financial transaction, you will receive a percentage share of a huge sum of money.

This scam often involves not-too-subtle pulling of the heartstrings, for instance claiming that the protagonist is a refugee from a current warzone, or requires help for a life-threatening medical condition. You merely have to help facilitate the movement of this giant sum, and that involves paying an administration fee of, say, a couple of thousand pounds. This scam works because the admin fee (the advance fee of the title) is just a fraction of the million or so you stand to receive, so it doesn't appear to be any kind of outlay at all. But that initial payment will be the first of many, if the fraudsters know what they're doing. In fact, the only direction that money ever flows is from you to the gang who are running the scam. As dodgepots go, the gangs who run this kind of scam are from the aisle marked 'DO NOT GO NEAR UNDER ANY CIRCUMSTANCES'. Accepting the invitation to help means that you'll lose your money, if you're lucky.

> As dodgepots go, the gangs who run this kind of scam are from the aisle marked 'DO NOT GO NEAR UNDER ANY CIRCUMSTANCES'.

If you're unlucky you can end up playing a game of hide and seek with a criminal enterprise in a country with which you're unfamiliar. I know, because in the course of an investigation I've done it, and while it was exhilarating and weirdly fun to spend time that way in Amsterdam, we got away with it by the skin of our teeth and no way would I choose to do it again.

Advance fee fraud comes in more flavours than jelly beans. It's been doing the rounds for hundreds of years in its different guises, but once again, it has some characteristics that are, if you look out for them, easy to spot. Anything unsolicited that offers you money or an opportunity to make money but requires your money to get at it, is, in the cold light of day, a nonsense. So let's keep the curtains drawn back and the windows open. Don't under any circumstances send money to anyone you don't know using untraceable transfer systems (Western Union springs to mind, but I'm sure there are others).

As Columbo might say, just one more thing: there is a troubling version of advanced fee fraud around today which offers financial loans. As personal debt in the UK reaches crisis levels, it's particularly appealing to those with bad credit history and escalating bills. Don't let them reel you in with this:

➜ Beware of loan offers that demand an administration fee that may appear refundable. Think about it: if they're loaning you money, why do they need money? If you do part with money for fees, don't pay any follow-up demands.

⬅ Check the loan firm you are dealing with is regulated by the Financial Conduct Authority. You can look it up on the Financial Services Register, which is a public record of those individuals and companies. Use the details from the FSR to contact the company.

Matt Nav

OK. Amsterdam. Being idiots, we accepted invitations from two separate advance fee fraud gangs to meet up in a park in the Dutch capital. We arranged one meeting in the morning and one in the afternoon. We took a giant Kiwi security guy called Phil with us and posed as businessmen. In the morning I decided to pretend to be a bit mad and faced down the scam artist who met us, expecting to get his hands on the couple of thousand I didn't have in my briefcase. He wanted us to go on a car journey with him, which seemed like a really bad idea, but once I started menacingly reciting all my favourite football teams, he decided I was far too dangerous to deal with and left. Kiwi Phil said he counted another five gang members circling in the park.

In the afternoon we played it slightly differently. We told our contact that we had the money he wanted, but that it had been buried by Dutch colleagues somewhere in the park, and that we had been given a map to show its location. Out of the briefcase we pulled a map, drawn in crayon, featuring a single tree, a pond and an X between them to mark the spot. Amsterdam's Vondelpark is 120 acres of woodland and lakes. We made him measure and dig with a twig in several locations before we finally took pity and let him leave. Kiwi Phil, who was ex-NZ special forces and had infiltrated several criminal gangs at home, said it was by far the silliest thing he'd ever done. And you don't argue with Phil.

AUTHORISED PUSH PAYMENT (APP) FRAUD

This one is truly devastating, and serves to highlight how scams rely on pressure and time to shred your common sense. We really don't come across many more pressured situations than completing the purchase of a home, and there are fraudsters ready to take advantage of that desperately difficult time. Imagine putting the deposit down on your new home, only to find your life savings had been pocketed by scamsters who had hijacked your solicitor's online identity. Tragically it's even got its own nickname – 'Friday Afternoon Fraud' – because that's when so many property transactions complete.

This is how it happens: an email account is illegally accessed by hackers, and used to pose as a legitimate operation. But they do nothing at first, just observing communications to and fro until it's apparent that a client is about to transfer a major sum of dosh. That's when they send a different set of bank details from those used by the bona fide solicitor – along with a credible reason why you should use them. You have no reason at all to question it, since it's just the latest in a long line of correspondence

Matt Stat

APP fraud losses totalled £208 million across nearly 58,000 cases in the first six months of 2019.

with the same source. The bad news is that once the money lands in the account nominated by the thieves it will be whipped off to another, until all trace of it melts away. For this to work, their timing has to be immaculate. Sadly, this is one of the few scams where the 'Out Of The Blue Not For You' (OOTBNFY) advice doesn't really work. You'll feel every step of the way that it's an established, trusted professional company you're dealing with. It's virtually impossible to claw back the money, but there are ways to prevent this scam:

→ Telephone the company presenting an invoice using an independently verified number. Check the request and bank details are genuine, even if you are expecting it.

← Pay a small sum first, to make certain it is going to the right account, and only transfer large amounts when the correct destination has been confirmed.

Some banks have joined a scheme that will help some victims of APP fraud. Eight banks across 17 brands have signed up at time of writing,, and contribute to a central pot that provides re-imbursement. It pays out to customers deemed blame-free in fraud debacles. But that's still not a guarantee that you will ever see your money again.

ROMANCE SCAMS (CATFISHING)

I was saying at the beginning that scams can take away much more than money. Romance scams can cause damage to a person's self-esteem that's hard to recover from.

They're also enjoying a bit of a boom. Why? Well, perhaps because in the last decade or so hooking up with a partner on the internet has gone from a bit of a shameful secret to, well, the way things tend to get done. But starting your relationship remotely comes with hazards attached. You have to place trust, at least initially, in profile pictures and descriptions instead of a physical presence, and that gives scammers another layer to hide behind. However, put your love goggles to one side, use some simple tools and romance scams can be spotted, deflected and kicked in the seat of the pants.

> Put your love goggles to one side.

Catfishers generally need an excuse not to be able to meet up. Be particularly suspicious if your new boo is working overseas, perhaps in the military or as an overseas aid worker, for instance. Of course, this hardly makes them less attractive. Then, look at how quickly the

> *You think you're cementing the relationship, forming a bond based on trust. You're sending money to a stranger who, in all likelihood, has four or five fake relationships on the go.*

relationship ramps up. Has it been an indecent sprint from small talk to wedding talk? Why?

The close

This is all leading to the close, often in the form of an emergency or a desperate need to come home and see you. And the beauty is that YOU can be the saviour, wiring much-needed funds (he or she is wealthy, but indisposed) to get them out of a fix in a warzone or airport somewhere. This will be the first, but not last of these transactions, as you get reeled in to the drama and excitement of it all. You think you're cementing the relationship, forming a bond based on trust. You're sending money to a stranger who, in all likelihood, has four or five fake relationships on the go.

People don't tend to talk about romance scams because they feel so foolish, but there's often another kicker: the internet now gives people the ability to share pictures of themselves – intimate pictures, which they fear could be used to blackmail them later. That's another reason to clam up. I only hope that as finding love on the internet is more common and accepted, people will feel they can be honest about when it's gone wrong.

Of course, anyone who's looking for love has to lay themselves open to a certain degree. It's the nature of the thing. But you also need to dot the Is and cross the Ts. If you're using a dating site, check what it offers in terms of traceability, protection etc. Do a Google reverse image search on your Prince or Princess Charming (copy their pic into the search engine). It's amazing what you can find: it may turn out that they're nothing like what they say they are, or that other people have been stung using the same pic. Keep your webcam offline, don't share too much online – definitely nothing raunchy – and NEVER, EVER send anyone money.

Matt Stat

There was a 64 per cent increase in romance scams in the first half of 2019, according to banking group UK Finance, which says £7.9 million was lost by 935 people, with just £500,000 being recovered on behalf of victims. With luck, that increase is partly due to more people overcoming a natural embarrassment and reporting their losses.

HOLIDAY FRAUD

Booking a holiday has never been easier. Getting defrauded while booking a holiday, however, has also never been easier. I used to regularly report on big package holiday companies who had let down their customers and failed to give people what they'd been promised. Well, as we saw with Thomas Cook, those big companies are under more pressure than ever as people choose to book their flights and accommodation independently. While doing that can free you up and save you some money, it can also leave you wide open. Let's deal with the two big ticket items separately: flights and accommodation.

Flights

Are you really booking your flights with who you think you are? Millions of pounds every year go on fake flights which land you and your family standing in the airport with a bogus ticket to nowhere. Wearing flip-flops. 57 per cent of all holiday scams involve fake flights. The key here is to look out for website addresses that are close-but-no-cigar to the authentic provider's. The address might add a word here or there to look legit but in fact redirect you away from the real biz. For instance, tui.co.uk gets me to the Tui site. As I write now, any number of variants of the name tuidirect are available as websites to anyone who fancies flogging fake flights to folk. That's a warning, not advice. Also, check that the http that precedes the domain has an 's' after it, making it https://. It gives a degree of reassurance that the site is what it says it is, and won't be prone to someone getting in the middle of the flow of info between you and the company.

Accommodation

Did I mention Google Reverse Image Search earlier? Why yes, I believe I did! It will never be more useful than when you're booking accommodation overseas, expecting to flop onto the pillow you saw on the website when you booked. Accommodation booking websites like Airbnb and booking.com are plastered with reassurances about what will happen if your holiday home is not as advertised. But they won't be there holding your hand when you're standing in front of an empty lot, or when you find another family enjoying their fortnight instead of you. Before you part with any money, however pressured you are, reverse image search where you're going. Do the pictures have the same address as you've been given? Also check on Google Maps on satellite. Drop the little yellow man in on street view. Can he spot your property? It's worth looking at the reviews on the site as well. How far do they go back? Do the names feel a bit, you know, made up? If there are 150 positive reviews over a six-week period, which all say things like 'Gary is a wonderful host. I would recommend dealing with Barry every time. His weclome (sic) pack made us feel right at home. Thank you Larry!', then perhaps it's worth looking elsewhere.

When it comes to booking accommodation, here are some beach-ball basics:

→ If you're using a booking website, don't be lured into paying for a holiday outside the site's own system. Odds-on you'll lose the protection it offers.

← Wherever possible, use a credit card to get Section 75 protection (see p. 23). You may need it. Using Paypal, or a wire transfer service, funded by your credit card, doesn't give you that same protection.

→ Check for other protections, e.g. ATOL, ABTA, and cross-check any registration numbers with those bodies independently. They're easy to fake.

← Call the owners directly. Get a bricks and mortar address for them if you can. If it's a hotel, but you're using a booking site, call reception and check they've got your booking long before you leave your home.

TICKETING SCAMS

When I started going to gigs, to stand a chance of getting a ticket, you literally had to queue up with hundreds of other smelly teens outside the venue, sometimes on a weekday, often at 9am. How far we've come! Now to stand a chance of getting a ticket for a gig, you either have to invest in software that clicks BUY NOW a thousand times a second on your behalf, or pay four times the asking price to a secondary selling site. Progress!

OK, I may be exaggerating, but sometimes it does feel like the people who really love music or theatre are now the least likely to get tickets direct. Tickets for even mildly popular acts and festivals seem to sell out in seconds, and as a result, desperate fans can get caught up in all sorts of dodgy side-alleys and end up paying exorbitant prices to people they've never met, and frankly, shouldn't trust.

With hot tickets for festivals and theatre productions selling out in minutes, it's easy to get swept up in the frenzy that follows. Craving entry to the gig, you are prepared to pay high prices to a seller to make your dreams come true. But you are putting yourself at risk of paying big money and still being stranded outside. It's not right that we should be looking back to the days of long queues and ticket touts with a misty-eyed nostalgia, but in some ways what we've got now is worse. It's often a real shot in the dark buying tickets online, whether from auction sites or third-party resellers. Some of them offer money-back protections, but just like a holiday, that's not much reassurance if you've travelled two hours to get there with kids who MUST see Justin Bieber before he hits 50.

The advice here is simple, but not entirely helpful. I understand the need to get to see your favourite artist, but without a shakeup of the entire market, people are going to struggle to do it without putting themselves at risk.

→ If AT ALL possible, buy direct from the venue or promoter.

← Ask for seat and block numbers before you buy. If the seller won't share, walk away.

→ Get tickets in your hand as soon as you can before you make travel arrangements. Verify with promoters that you've got real tickets.

← Buy on a credit card so if it goes wrong, you're wearing your scam-proof hat and coat.

Matt Nav

Secondary ticket sellers. A curse on them, quite frankly. They claim they are just facilitating the market for fans to sell to other fans, but their critics say they've allowed ticket touts to deal in hundreds of tickets at a time from the comfort of an armchair. I've reported over and over again on sites that are happy to carve out their percentage of hugely inflated prices, but when it all goes Wang Chung, their protections aren't worth a thing. Some artists have worked hard to get tickets directly into the hands of their fans. Ed Sheeran, for instance, has said that fans with resold tickets will be turned away. There are also some sites which cap resale values to 10 per cent of face value, but if you're a hardened armchair tout, surrounded by credit cards and laptops, are you going to bother with them, knowing that there are other sites allowing you to charge fans ten times that to see the mighty Michael Bublé? I stood outside an Ed Sheeran gig and met some old-fashioned touts who were disgusted with the secondary sites. 'At least we stand here in the wet and cold to make our money,' they said. Yep, genuine heroes, fellas.

TECH SCAMS

Right, I'm going to throw some nerdy terms at you now, but don't be alarmed. They're all versions of the same thing. Phishing, Vishing, Pharming and Smishing are not coastal towns in Denmark, but ways that scammers are trying to get to you in your home using the tech devices that are supposed to make life easier. Good news: they are all firmly kicked into touch using the OOTBNFY maxim.

Phishing

Phishing is fraud by email. The email seems to be from a reputable source and asks you to press a hyperlink to resolve some urgent issue or other, or even just to verify information. That click places you in the lap of the scammer who will then harvest your personal information with ease. If you're scanning your email quickly the imitation might have you fooled, but look closely and spelling errors, clunky phrases, odd idioms and fake email addresses that are one or two letters short of the real thing start to stand out. Typically, the bad guys will use condensed links to mask the real destination. If you're cyber-savvy, it only takes a moment to copy that link and drop it into a URL decoder, available online. Even if you're a cyber-dolt you can roll a mouse over the link to get a clearer picture. Don't forget, a genuinely secure page will be distinguished by an extra 's' in the URL, i.e. https://. The address bar may also change colour while a padlock appears in the corner of your browser bar. But in any event, the rule of thumb is always, don't press the hyperlink. If you do by mistake, disconnect from the internet as quickly as possible. Back up your files. Scan your computer with anti-virus software, and then change passwords for email, bank and other accounts that may have been held on that computer, using another machine that's not been affected. Pain in the buffer, right? Best not to click.

Vishing

Vishing is similar, but over the phone. Voice phishing, I suppose. It's all about getting you to share your bank details, PIN numbers and passwords. The fraudster will use whatever information they might already hold on you (date of birth, mother's maiden name, etc.) to persuade you that they are legit, and then ask you to confirm the rest. The story they'll tell you is often that your bank account has been compromised by an attempted fraud, and needs to be reset, or that money needs to be moved to a safe account. A couple of stinky vishing techniques that can change the flavour slightly:

➡ Number spoofing. Crims can now make caller ID on your phone show whatever they want, including the genuine number of your bank. It's enough to convince a lot of customers that they're being called by their bank. This is, by the way, a massive backward step, phone companies. Thanks.

⬅ Keypad entry. Crims also know that a lot of phone banking involves you entering passcodes as a security measure. You may think you're sticking in your PIN number without anyone knowing, but they'll hear and decode that number at the other end, and can use it to get money out. Of course they'll need your card first…

➡ … and that's where courier fraud comes in. Your card is compromised? We'll send someone round to collect it! We now have your card and your PIN number and, therefore, access to all the money in your account. Thank you and goodnight!

Banks will never ask for your details over the phone. If you have any doubt about someone who's calling you claiming to be from your bank, call them back using the number on the back of your debit card or statement.

Matt Nav

Another variant of vishing is the 'Microsoft Scam'. This is when an OOTBNFY computer specialist calls up saying that your machine is infected with a virus and he needs to get in to clean it (out of your money). I really don't advise that you see how much of this guy's time you can waste by getting him to help with turning on the computer while you actually do the ironing. I've done this. You run the risk of making him very, very angry indeed, and as a result you might just die laughing, so please, whatever you do, don't do that.

Matt Stat

In 2018 Microsoft reported that over half of all their customers had been targeted by a tech support scam.

Pharming

Pharming is also fraud by email: taking over your inbox and
pointing you to fake sites. An infested email that plants
a virus in your computer's address book is to blame. It's
slightly rarer than phishing, but it can nonetheless affect
lots of people. If a familiar webpage you are visiting looks
substantially different, your own address book may be
compromised. It's time to run some anti-virus software
and flush that sucker out.

Smishing

Smishing is fraud by text. SMS phishing, I suppose, using
the logic of vishing. All the same rules apply. Don't
respond at all, even if you are invited to stop the texts
arriving, because this proves the phone is live and you
could be charged at unfeasibly high rates for the message.
The best option is to delete the text, unread, and have a
cup of tea.

In fact, a lot of the same rules apply for dealing with these
four horsemen of the cyberpocalypse:

> A genuine bank will never contact you out of the blue
> and will never request your PIN number or password.
> Nor will it ask you to transfer money from one
> account to another.

2 No matter how alarming an electronic message, don't click on the links it contains.

3 Don't feel rushed by a caller or an email. A bank would never ask you to make strategic financial moves on the hop. SCDC!

4 Make contact with your bank on a number you trust, like the one on the back of your payment card, to find out if there really is an issue. But don't do so immediately on the phone in your hand after a suspect call, in case the fraudster is keeping the line open. Wait five minutes or, better still, use a different phone.

5 Install security on to your computer to defend it from viruses and hackers and make sure it is regularly updated.

MAIL FRAUD

Remember the old posty? Well, it may surprise you to learn that in many parts of the UK letters are still delivered ALMOST EVERY DAY. Just because you don't have a computer doesn't mean you won't be scam fodder, as there are still heaps of old-school swindles in existence.

Via the Royal Mail, dodgy letters can be popped through the front door of your home from anywhere in the world, and it is the elderly that seem most vulnerable. Anyone who responds to the architects of such scams is then put on a 'suckers list', earmarking them for mailsack-loads of more creepy and calculating correspondence. Beware of anything that looks like it comes from:

→ A lottery, particularly operating overseas.

← Someone who claims they can see into the future. They can't, but they can see you coming.

→ Someone who wants to trace your family history. You could end up sharing exactly the sort of details with them (date of birth, mother's maiden name) that can help them get at your savings, and leave you no closer to knowing if you're related to Danny Dyer.

← Debt recovery agents. Now obviously, if you have debts, you have to pay them, but for many people, a letter carrying the threat of court action is enough to make them send payment, even if they're not sure what they owe for. I've seen many postal scams that take advantage of this fact.

→ Parcel delivery notifications for parcels you weren't expecting. This one works particularly well at Christmas, when SantAmazon is at his busiest anyway. The card poked through your door offers a number to call to make fresh arrangements. Expect to spend a long time on an expensive premium phone line trying to rearrange redelivery.

Seriously, junk mail can make people's lives a misery, and it disproportionately affects the older generation, who on the whole, are more comfortable receiving things through the post than online. I've met people whose lives have been decimated by junk mail, depriving them of their savings and dignity. If there's someone you care about, just keep an eye out for the signs they've made it onto a list of targets: a growing pile of windowed and badged letters each delivery, often combined with a growing sense of secrecy and anxiety.

Matt Nav

Joining opt-out services is another piece of advice that I often give, knowing that it's only half an answer. The Telephone and Mail Preferential Services (TPS and MPS) are all very well and good, but they really only work to cut out unsolicited contact from honest companies who play by the rules and sign up to those services. It's therefore a bit like taking out an insurance policy against getting kicked in the shins by Mary Berry. The only really positive effect is that if you do sign up to either the TPS or MPS and still receive an unsolicited call or letter, you can pretty much guarantee it's from a bunch of dodgepots, as they won't have signed up to the scheme. In any case, OOTBNFY still provides you with the best protection of all.

Hooray for me!

IDENTITY THEFT

A lot of the above scams involve a degree of identity theft. People assume some element of your persona, whether it's your bank details or your address, run up debts and then run away. If you're a dodgepot, it's a lot easier than being yourself.

Get the right personal details and you can open bank accounts, obtain credit, claim benefits, sign up to loans and even get a passport, all without consequences. The ID thief won't be paying back the loan, so the burden falls on you to explain why it wasn't your fault. Your credit rating, your reputation and even a criminal record could be at stake if they start claiming benefits on your behalf.

But it's alarmingly simple to take on someone else's financial persona. You can start with small beginnings and details as basic as your name and address. Add to that a passport or driving license and you've got a wealth of details that can be culled and used against you. While it's going on you won't have a clue unless you've been keeping an eye out and protecting yourself like this:

➜ Make sure all your rubbish, recycled and other, is free of anything that gives away name, address, date of birth or age. Shred or burn anything that indicates who you bank with, your mortgage or pension provider, or who your employer might be.

← Check over your bank account on a weekly basis if possible. It's easier to remember payments from the last week. If you get a monthly paper statement, give it a thorough going over to make sure that you recognise every payment, however small. Scammers often test the water with small payments to see if they're noticed.

→ If you receive notification of benefit payments in your name, obviously, contact the paying authority straight away. Failure to do so might make them think that you're complicit in the fraud.

← Got a letter from a solicitor or bailiff letters trying to recover a debt that isn't yours? Don't pay it, but also don't ignore it as a mistake. Someone else could be running up debts in your name.

→ If you start receiving packages that you didn't order, don't assume that Santa made a mistake. It might be that someone else is ordering big ticket items and hoping to intercept them while you're at work or away on holiday.

← Cancel lost cards immediately, shred all financial information before binning it and keep your vital financial details in a locked drawer at home, so intruders can't clean out your accounts as well as your belongings.

CRASH
FOR CASH

This one is utterly ruthless, risking not just your money and confidence, but your physical wellbeing too. You've probably seen how car insurance premiums have gone through the roof in recent years. Well, this is in no small part due to the emergence of organised criminal gangs who orchestrate car crashes to fleece the insurance system, and you, out of thousands.

A typical scenario: there's an unwritten rule that in the event of a bumper-to-bumper crash, the driver behind is generally at fault for not maintaining a safe distance. What crash-for-cashers often do is either disable their brake lights or even reverse into another car in a queue of traffic. As soon as the collision takes place, you're surrounded by helpful witnesses (fellow crims) all adamant that you

There's an unwritten rule that in the event of a bumper-to-bumper crash, the driver behind is generally at fault.

were at fault. Another variant ('Flash For Cash') is for the other driver to indicate that he is politely letting you out, ceding right of way, only to T-bone you. You know what happened. But it's your word against that of the rapidly forming crowd of stooges.

However it proceeds from there on, it's not pretty. Resist a claim on your insurance and you could find yourself wide open to cash payment after payment to put things right. But go the insurance route and the pay-outs can be even bigger as so-called victims look for compensation for personal injury, vehicle damage, loss of earnings, vehicle recovery and car hire. The gangs involved can set up their own repair shops, and get doctors and solicitors onside to maximise their take and help the claims go through.

There's also evidence those who stage accidents funnel the money into organised crime, including the purchase of illegal weapons and human trafficking. And of course, it's putting lives at risk on the road. If you're in a crash and it doesn't feel right:

➡ Take notes and photos at the scene. Try to find witnesses outside those who offer themselves, and ideally, footage.

⬅ Insist on calling the police.

➡ Report it to your insurance company, along with any suspicions you have.

← Never part with money on the roadside. Not only are you being scammed but you are being drawn into committing an offence, by not reporting an accident to your insurance company.

→ Install a dash cam, which will prove your version of events.

Matt Stat

According to the Insurance Fraud Bureau, £340 million a year is lost to 'crash for cash' fraud. No wonder our premiums have gone up. Some estimates reckon that criminal crashers are responsible for an average £50 hike in our premiums.

PRESSURE SELLING

Is this a scam? Some people regard selling as an art, and pressure selling as a distillation of that art. Selling is certainly a big part of culture in the US, celebrated in films and books, the preserve of big characters and made to seem worthy of, at the very least, grudging respect. But I just don't see it that way.

Over 20 years on *Rogue Traders* I've sat in silence and watched pressure selling taking place in the front rooms of houses we've hired expressly for that purpose. In our scenario the targets of these scams are brilliant actresses we've booked to sit, sometimes for hours on end, and receive a barrage of lies, threats, scare tactics and mounting attritional pressure to part with money, but I'm aware that the rest of the time they're ordinary men and women in their seventies or eighties. Your mum or dad, grandpa or grandma. As a result, I'm clear that what I've witnessed aren't the actions of loveable rogues, or an inevitable result of living in a consumerist society. I think it's criminal bullying, plain and simple. It's dishonest and exploitative and ultimately avoidable. But it continues to take place every day in front rooms across the country, and again, the results are terrible, decimating the savings of those on limited resources, and dividing families through guilt and shame. So let's make sure we can recognise it and steer clear.

Typically the first contact will be OOTBNFY in the form of a leaflet through the door or a cold call on the phone. However, this isn't always the case. Sometimes you might find an advert in a local paper for the thing that you're already thinking of buying, whether it's a mobility scooter, an orthopaedic bed, damp-proofing or that old favourite, double glazing. It's that beautiful moment of serendipity when your requirements could be fulfilled by someone who has just the thing you need. They might even be in the middle of a special offer! As a stroke of luck, a designer may be in your area right now! They may be able to offer a free, no-obligation survey/questionnaire/estimate for you. This is all, as they say, gravy. It's designed to get someone inside your home, and in the world of pressure selling that's very, very important.

Things change when you're being sold to in your home. Without knowing it, we subconsciously start treating people as guests rather than purely as salespeople, as we would in their shop. Getting people out of our home is also a lot harder than simply walking out of a shop and saying, 'I'll think about it. See ya!' That's why there are laws designed to protect people who make decisions about buying stuff in their own homes (see pp. 18–20). These laws are often completely ignored by pressure selling outfits.

So it's time for your pressure seller to arrive. Expect them to be punctual, friendly and well-presented. Anything else wouldn't get them any commission. Then settle in, because chances are it's going to be a long old ride. Here, in brief, is a classic pressure sales routine, in roughly the order it will happen:

1 Ding dong! Hello! Sit down. A chat about you. Your life, family, history.

2 A chat about the seller. Their life, family, history. It's possible there will be pictures of their children at this stage. You are now friends, especially if they have a cup of tea in their hands.

3 A discussion of your needs. If we are talking about something with medical implications, like a bed or chair, expect a bit of pseudo-medical nonsense gained from watching a couple of episodes of Grey's Anatomy (subdural haematoma, CBC, Chem 7, etc.).

4 A demonstration of the quality and benefits of the product. Again, expect slightly irrelevant but eye-catching demonstrations of, for instance, the effect of vibrations on a small jar of rice, or pouring water onto a brick (I have witnessed both of these).

5 There now follows a linking of your specific needs to the benefits demonstrated, through a series of questions designed purely to elicit the answer 'Yes'. For instance: 'You said you'd like to cut down your heating bills. If I could show you how to do that, you'd be interested, wouldn't you?' The key for the seller here is to get the Yes count as high as possible.

6 No mention of the price yet.

7 That's because we're about to mention price! Just three hours in, and we're coming to the meat of the matter. But here's a guarantee: the first price your salesperson comes up with will be way, way too much. Think of a number. Double it. Add a nought. You're halfway there. We're into the price conditioning phase, designed to make you think you're getting a bargain! That price is about to come tumbling down for any number of reasons: 'You're part of a promotional deal!' 'I'm taking a cut in my commission.' 'We're overstocked in this model.' The price can fall by up to half at this stage. But we're not done yet.

8 If it's still a no, we revisit the 'Yes' questions from point 5, because you, the customer, have clearly forgotten how to say yes. 'We agreed that this would be good for you, didn't we?' 'You told me you wanted to save money on your heating, didn't you?' The effect of this is to remove barriers to the sale, and by implication, establish that if the only obstacle is price, then that's no obstacle at all.

9 Another price drop, perhaps even facilitated by a call back to the office. This time, expect the discount to be time-limited – only if you sign today, otherwise the offer disappears. This one is not just immoral, it's actually outlawed in the marvellous Consumer

Protection from Unfair Trading Regulations of 2008 (see p. 16). In your face, cheap suit!

10 If you're still holding out at this stage, things could get nasty. Threats, accusations of time-wasting, pleas of poverty or repercussions if the sale isn't made, I've heard all of these. A desire to consult family members at this stage is like poison for a pressure seller. 'They're just after your inheritance!' is one line I've heard regularly.

11 If there's still no sign of pen and contract meeting, return to point 5. And repeat until everybody faints or falls asleep.

I'm making light of a process that is designed to reduce people, many of them elderly, to the point of least resistance. Many of them will sign because they no longer have the strength to get the seller out of their house by any other means. Through embarrassment they will then keep schtumm throughout the period during which they have the right to cancel under the Consumer Contract Regulations (see p. 19), until they take delivery of their overpriced and under-appropriate item or service to serve as a lasting reminder of how they got it wrong. It's a miserable state of affairs that we somehow allow to continue despite upgrades to the law and simple common sense.

EMPLOYMENT SCAMS

If you're looking for work or for a change of career direction, you should be full of confidence, willing and ready to commit to a new venture, whatever it throws at you. That's what employers love to see. But not as much as fraudsters, who will harness that enthusiasm to, without putting too fine a point on it, do you up like a kipper.

Employment scams are often variants on advance fee fraud (see p. 36). You'll hand over a sum in exchange for the promise of work or opportunity. The real tragedy is that, for people seeking work, those funds are often borrowed from friends or family members who want the best for them. Being unemployed and unable to contribute brings one kind of shame, being in debt as well can be really damaging to a family. Look out for the following warning signs:

→ Overseas jobs – particularly with idyllic descriptions – are difficult to scrutinise properly. If the position requires you to pay an up-front fee for training, visas, immigration or security clearance, then start asking some serious questions. If the organisation really wants you, they'll consider covering these costs.

- Phone interviews are commonplace, certainly initially. Phone interviews on premium rate lines (070-, 09-) are to be avoided like Piers Morgan in an otherwise empty pub.

- Working from home seems like an ideal solution for many hardworking parents but the sought-after job can be a cover for money laundering. There's also often an up-front fee involved. Double whammy.

- Having apparently landed a job, you might be asked for detailed bank account information, which will then be used to empty your account.

- CVs are great to give to genuine potential employers. Many will also contain everything needed for a pretty successful identity theft. Make sure your CV isn't giving someone the keys to your bank account.

- Check the name of the business with Companies House and make contact through the numbers given there to find out if the role you've applied for really is on offer. When the job offer is overseas, call the country's embassy in the UK to check the cost of visas. If the answer doesn't match that given already, that indicates double dealing. Remember, you can always insist on making your own travel and accommodation arrangements in order to flush out a scammer.

Matt Nav

According to Action Fraud, it's young people who are most at risk of employment fraud. Those aged between 18 and 25 are likely to be targeted, losing on average £4,000.

The first doorstep bust I ever did was an employment scam. A dodgy company in the North West was offering the chance to manage your own pub for a mere £5,000. What in fact happened to applicants, once they'd paid their money, was that, under the guise of 'on-the-job-training', they would effectively become unpaid labour in a pub for as long as the arrangement lasted. The bosses, meanwhile, would pocket the fee, and, one assumes, also collect a fee for their efforts from the landlord. I ended up pointing this out to them through the crack in the door I'd maintained by inserting my Doc Marten boot as they closed it. The two directors' combined weight behind the door totalled, I estimate, around 40 stone. A sturdy door, it was four inches open at the bottom, and virtually closed at the top. To make good my escape I was therefore required to unlace my boot and leave it for collection at a later date.

I could go on, and on, and on about scams, and this isn't anything like a definitive guide to fraud. The nature of the beast is that it's constantly evolving to bring in new ideas. Handily, though, as you'll have seen, they're usually new riffs on the same old songs, and some major themes emerge which, if you identify them early enough, mean you stand a fair chance of dodging a bullet. One last time…

OUT OF THE BLUE? NOT FOR YOU!

chapter
three

Is the customer still king?

Shopping

1947. Imagine the scene: A shop where you serve YOURSELF! No-one running up and down a ladder to fetch a box of cornflour. When it happened, people threw their hands in the air and predicted the end of the world as we knew it. And they were right.

Supermarkets, shopping malls, self-service tills, Amazon. The pace of change in the world of shopping has been supersonic. But is the customer still king? Well, as you'll see, your rights have had to sprint just to keep up, and it's as much about protecting yourself these days. For this chapter, there will be a fair bit of flipping backward and forward to the legal pages, so make sure your thumbs are nicely hydrated. Here we go!

SUPERMARKETS

Britain is now dominated by the big four: Tesco, Sainsbury's, Asda and Morrisons, which each take up between 27 and 10 per cent of market share (as of 2019). The market is balancing out a bit, though, as the next four, Aldi, Co-op, Lidl and Waitrose, all weigh in between 5–8 per cent.

It's fiercely competitive. In 2002 Safeway was the country's fourth biggest supermarket chain. Two years later it had been swallowed up by Morrisons, a much smaller rival. A similar story for Gateway, which became Somerfield and then morphed into the Co-op. This kind of dogfight should be good news for us as customers. I'm going to underline should.

Well, yes and no. Sometimes prices are appealingly low, and other times they are downright, invisibly pumped. Supermarkets love working the big, big data they have on us to pull us in with headline prices, then kick us where it hurts in our blind spots. For shoppers, this is only going to get harder to work around thanks to the phenomenon of dynamic pricing. It's already in online retail, but supermarkets are next, so over the next few years expect to see price labels replaced by digital readouts that can flick up or down second-by-second in real time. The

> *Supermarkets love working the big, big data they have on us to pull us in with headline prices, then kick us where it hurts.*

extreme of this is that the price could change not just based on what competitors are doing, but based on what the chain knows about us individually through our loyalty cards, shopping history, etc. Drive a Jag? Your loaf costs double, mush, but this delicious panettone is half price right now! I find this creepy. Many people accept it's the way it's going to be. I think there's a big price to be placed on transparency.

Deals and discounts

For the moment, the big draws come in the shape of discounts: things like the Buy One Get One Free, or BOGOF, as it's affectionately known. If the product is toilet rolls, that's great. You know you will get around to using them and they won't pass a sell-by date in storage. But if you buy a bag of satsumas a week, and they go off in a week, why would you buy two bags? Unless you have a friend who's vitamin C deficient. You have to watch BOGOFs like a hawk, for three reasons. First, there's no guarantee the offer is a good one. Sometimes the original price of the product has been upped to make the saving look more impressive. Secondly, look at the small print to ensure it's not cheaper to buy a single alternative. Thirdly, cheaper rates writ large in the store aisles may themselves be out of date. A *Watchdog* investigation in 2017 revealed when products were put through the till there was no sign of the promised reduction. That's because the promotion had ended but still appeared as current in the relevant displays. Of course, what the till says, goes. Unless you notice in time and make a fuss. Multi-buys fall into the same category. We've found six-packs that are more expensive than buying six of the solo item. There's no real intrigue here. Stores are changing their prices all the time, and don't always tie up one offer with another.

Matt Nav

Which? magazine carried out a fascinating survey recently. Despite the common belief that food prices are going up and sizes are shrinking, it turns out that, certainly compared with 30 years ago, quite the opposite is true. Across 16 different common foods, 2016 prices were cheaper in real terms than their 1988 equivalents, the only exception was white fish. Go back further and it's even more impressive. In the 1950s we spent a whopping third of our income on food. By 1974 this had gone down to 24 per cent. We've never had it so good!

Here's a tip direct from my mum. Be a (friendly) sticker stalker. Find out who the supermarket's yellow ticket person is. Track their movements. Over the course of a few trips you can narrow down their runs to a few minutes. That's the time to attack, particularly if you shop daily, or every couple of days. Then STRIKE!!! Follow them like a lost sheep, and plan your menu that evening based on what they ticket. Why shouldn't smoked haddock be accompanied by twiglets and jam? No good reason I can think of. Although timings vary – with 24-hour stores being the most difficult to predict – most supermarkets start to mark down first after lunch and then in the evening, about an hour or two before closing. The best bargains usually appear prior to a bank holiday. On a slow day, you might buy luxury items for a fraction of the usual cost, so put anything you can't use immediately into the freezer for another day. And Christmas puddings should ONLY be bought in January. They last for two years, people.

For regular purchases, know your prices, and shop per 100g, just like Grandma would have if she knew metric. Products change their recipe and shrink all the time,

> *The best bargains usually appear prior to a bank holiday.*

particularly since ingredients became more expensive in the last few years. Beware old products with a new look. Biscuits marketed as 'thins' are a prime example. How appealing and dainty! But typically 50 per cent more expensive. There's a chocolate/biscuit ratio thing going on there, but let's not get bogged down.

Don't go shopping when you are hungry, especially when there's an in-store bakery. Be aware that supermarkets know how tall you are, and that you don't like to bend down. As a result, they'll put the things they want you to buy at eye-level. The things you really want which are virtually the same but cheaper are down by your ankles. Do a bit of trolley yoga (troga?), flex from the middle and save yourself a packet.

Labelling

We are unduly influenced by subliminal words and phrases that mean nothing. The following can be disregarded and mistrusted: 'quality', 'farmhouse', 'natural', 'family-sized', 'local', 'whole', 'superfood', 'multi-grain', 'gourmet', 'select' and 'premium'. My personal favourite is 'fresh', particularly when it's applied to eggs. As no-one wants to buy rotten ones, I've always kind of assumed any eggs on a supermarket shelf would be fresh.

For their predecessor, the chicken, watch out for phrases like 'trusted farms', 'trusted farmers' and 'reared with care'.

> *'Healthy' means nothing, as everything is subject to how you use it.*

'Higher welfare standards' sometimes appears but it is unlikely that chicken has had treatment in anyway superior to its neighbour on the next shelf. All these terms imply some kind of trade standard, but in reality the words mean very little.

'Healthy' means nothing, as everything is subject to how you use it. A cucumber is often regarded as 'healthy', but freeze it and it becomes a lethal weapon. Much more useful are traffic light indicators of how much fat, saturated fat, sugar and salt are in the product. A BBC investigation in 2019 discovered supermarket food marked as a healthier choice or even as a diet food exceeded recommended levels. When it comes to protecting your health, go with numbers, not fudgy little phrases that don't mean much.

There are some useful symbols to look out for, including Red Tractor and RSPCA Assured, which are properly related to living standards. Free range and organic labels indicate the chickens have had access to the outdoors, with space to move around in, natural light and some manner of enrichment in their otherwise limited lives. These labels don't favour faster growing breeds.

Out-of-date food has caused a lot of controversy over the last few years. To be clear, it's really not a good idea to eat food that is properly off, but we do end up wasting food that can be salvaged. Hard cheeses, for instance, if mouldy, can be saved with a bit of skillful knife work. It's also a case of knowing your way around those labels again. If it bears the words 'use by', then make a point of getting the food gone by that date for the sake of your health. But 'sell by' and 'best before' are advisories, and the food is very likely to be safe and tasty for some time after that date.

Supermarket own brands: are they really produced by the same big names you'll find at eye-level and then re-badged? Well, maybe. Both supermarkets and food manufacturers are notoriously coy about revealing what comes from where. If they are quizzed about it, the makers claim anything they make for supermarkets has a different recipe from their own premium products. What's kind of exciting is the cheeky lookee-likees that Aldi and Lidl have developed. It may well be a case of having to do a taste test at home as it will nail down whether you prefer branded over basic. Definitely don't fall for the idea that it must taste better if you pay more. You could save hundreds of pounds a year.

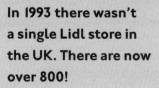

Matt Nav

OK, having said it's wonderful to see Burpack butter and McBitty's biscuits hit the shelves of low-cost supermarkets, that cheeky mimicry takes on a whole other side when they target small manufacturers and innovators. In April 2019 I met Cara Sayer, a brilliant woman who, from her own brain cells, had spent several years developing a sunshade for baby buggies which was that rare thing – a great idea, well executed. Imagine her despair when she saw that Aldi started selling an almost identical, but poorer quality version for half the price. Without the resources to take them to court, she's had to take it on the chin. But amazing how a firm can turn from cheeky little disruptor into schoolyard bully when there's money in it. Talk about throwing shade!

Matt Stat

In 1993 there wasn't a single Lidl store in the UK. There are now over 800!

Packaging

It used to be the case that loose fruit and veg were cheaper than packaged options. It's not always true now but always check – then buy loose because it saves on packaging and we've all got to do our bit for the environment. Arguably, supermarkets are not doing their bit, with a study in 2019 suggesting that nearly half the wrapping used by supermarkets could not be recycled. Which? broke down packaging into component parts in a shopping basket containing 46 items. On average just 52 per cent of the material used could be recycled in domestic bins.

You might be surprised to hear this as you cautiously pick your way through products to find the ones whose packages are best recycled. But there are some pretty misleading recycling symbols out there now.

Perhaps most problematic is the green dot, holding two arrows in light and dark green within a circle. Looks like that's ripe for recycling, doesn't it? In fact it doesn't mean the packaging is recyclable, will be recycled or has been recycled. The yin and yang style symbol used in some European countries indicates the producer has made some financial contribution towards recycling in Europe. Greenwashing, as the phrase goes.

There are some pretty misleading recycling symbols out there.

Then there is the Möbius Loop, three arrows chasing one another in an impossible sequence and forming a triangle. It's a familiar sight and denotes that the item can be recycled but not that it will be readily accepted by local authorities. Sometimes there's a figure in the middle and that says how much recycled material has already been used. If the word PET appears beneath, with a number at the centre, then somebody who probably isn't you will know which type of plastic resin has been used. Aluminium is straightforward enough, with the letters 'alu' appearing in the middle of a circle, while a red magnet appears on the side of steel that can be recycled.

Look instead for a green square with a white, broken circle in the middle. It usually has the encouraging words 'widely recycled' underneath and may give other small font advice like 'rinse', or 'flatten, cap on'. Items to avoid are those on a black square with a white, broken circle in it which denotes the items is not yet recycled. Which begs the question, why is it being used?

Loyalty

As the war of the discounts rages, many of our big-name supermarkets have worked out that we need something more to keep us loyal. A points system with rewards or money off groceries has been the main draw since 1994 when Tesco launched its Clubcard. As mentioned above, whenever we use this it gives up loads of data about our

> *In essence, shop where you like, rather than holding out for a rainbow at the end of your checkout receipts.*

shopping habits, which is now crucially important to the big guns in shaping their strategy. That's the implicit deal: you show us what you're buying, where and when, and every year we'll pay for a trip for you all to Alton Towers or a portable barbecue. The downside for us as customers is that the points are worth exactly as much as the supermarkets decide they're worth, which could go up or down depending on how they're feeling. The offers that are there when you start collecting points may have disappeared by the time you come to redeem. In essence, shop where you like, rather than holding out for a rainbow at the end of your checkout receipts.

Resist the urge to join a supermarket savings scheme – where you pay in a sum weekly and withdraw it in the form of coupons before Christmas – as these are not protected in the UK, and if it collapsed you wouldn't be entitled to any money back. And really the only people receiving a Christmas gift with schemes like this are those at the top of these big businesses because it gives them free money for a bit. You're usually better off finding a savings account.

Online delivery

These guys are really motoring. In Summer 2019, Ocado recorded the biggest growth among all grocery stores, with an increase in sales of 12.5 per cent. It's not making a profit but then you feel that's part of the strategy, and investors don't seem to mind, as its share price is buoyant. You might have seen the lorries but you won't have seen the stores, because there aren't any. (Linked with Waitrose in the past, Ocado are now joining up with M&S but also provide other goods.) Ocado's different from the others because it only operates online, without having to sync up with troublesome shops which weren't necessarily designed to supply trucks day and night. Of course all of this has gone through the roof since COVID-19. Whether it's a permanent change, we'll have to see.

There are lots of advantages to grocery shopping online. It's a great way to control your spending because you're making your choices in a relaxed environment, without worrying too much about parking, the school run or whether the loo is out of order. Deliveries can be the same day if you play it right. Some customers are wary about receiving damaged goods but most operators are quick to rectify issues by providing an instant refund thanks to the power of new technology, so check the goods as they come through the door.

It's definitely worth checking out what offers are out there for first-time shoppers. I'd say it's not worth joining one, whatever your loyalties, unless there's a hefty discount to grab you. I'd also consider cycling through them until you've used up all the offers, by which time you may well have moved house and you can start all over again. At the end of the day, a banana will always be a banana. But a £35 discount on your first three online shops? That's something else.

Matt Nav

Perhaps the most off-putting drawback to having groceries delivered revolves around poor hygiene. *Watchdog* went undercover in one supermarket's delivery service to see how things were done. We found a troubling lack of training among drivers about how to keep crates and vans clean after spillages, with only a lucky few armed with cleaning kit to mop up messes. Delivery services have dropped plastic bags, which is great news for the environment. Not so great for the environment in which your food finds itself. Thoroughly wash everything you're going to eat, including the tops of cans and bottles. Work on the basis that all wrappings are dirty.

Sales promotions

OK, this doesn't just apply to supermarkets now. Just like BOGOF and multi-buys, there's no easier way to grab our attention than a neon yellow sign with 75 per cent off. Like Geminis and Virgos, these signs are inherently unreliable. (No, I don't believe in all that.)

In 2018 the Advertising Standards Authority, which monitors what's being said and done by salespeople, had more than 10,000 advertisements withdrawn because they were judged as potentially misleading. As customers, few of us have an idea of the pricing history of each object in the sale. We don't know when it hit its peak price, how long it stayed at that level or whether it has been subject to one long price erosion since the day it first appeared. But these details are crucial because without the context of previous prices, discounts mean nothing. There are also rules. For instance, discounting from a notional Recommended Retail Price (RRP) is a nonsense. The RRP can be totally made up to convince you you're getting a bargain. If you've come straight from the previous chapter on Scams, you'll recognise this as a form of 'price conditioning'. It's something that happens all the time in pressure selling (see p. 68).

There are also rules about the use of terms like 'up to' and 'from'. For example, a retailer can't boast that they're having a sale with items 'up to 70 per cent off' when only a small fraction of the goodies on offer fall into the 70 per cent category. It's the same with the words 'lowest price'. After trumpeting this, the retailer has to not only match other rock-bottom prices but must beat them. It's the difference between 'lowest prices guaranteed' – with opponents beaten – and 'lowest prices guarantee', which is more a price match.

As far as your rights are concerned, supermarkets are keenly aware that the loss of reputation that's risked in a customer dispute hugely outweighs the cost of, say, an additional bag of satsumas. Most operate a no-quibble guarantee on replacing things you don't like. If you don't like what's happening, keep moving up the management structure until you find someone who cares. Generally, they're pretty good.

> *As far as your rights are concerned, supermarkets are keenly aware that the loss of reputation that's risked in a customer dispute hugely outweighs the cost of, say, an additional bag of satsumas.*

Matt Nav

A family legend, now, which demonstrates supermarkets' desire to get things right. A few years back my mum bought our Christmas turkey from the store where she shopped at least every other day. When it came to prepare it on Christmas Eve, she didn't like the bird. She was convinced it had been frozen, despite being marked fresh. She called the store, who sent round their poultry manager to inspect it. He offered her a full refund, and the turkey to keep. Not good enough. He sourced another bird, for free, on top. No, said Mum, who knows her turkeys. The only solution? He had a turkey brought 30 miles by taxi from a legendary butcher's, after ringing round to find last-minute availability. On Christmas Eve. Madness? I'd say not, as the positive effect of my mum telling this story to everyone she knows, every Christmas, ever since, has proved it to be a bargain, whatever it cost. Clever chap.

HIGH STREET SHOPS

You've got to feel a bit for the old-fashioned shops that you actually go in with your feet. Rents are up and footfall's down, thanks to the addictive clickability of Amazon and the like. The mighty John Lewis is feeling the pinch from a 30 per cent business rates bill rise since 2017, amounting to an eye-watering £57 million in 2020 according to property advisory firm Colliers International. In retail John Lewis, House of Fraser and Marks & Spencer are high street bellwethers. As they ponder cutbacks and buyouts, property re-developers wait in the wings to buy up prime sites for housing. What they <u>can</u> offer is service, and that's what they're banking on to keep customers loyal. There's something to be said for that. You have to leave the house at some point.

Clothes

Although high-street clothes have never been cheaper to buy, there's a good chance that means that someone, somewhere is paying a high price. That was illustrated in 2013 when the Rana Plaza, a garment factory in Dhaka, Bangladesh, collapsed, causing the deaths of more than 1,100 people. A series of deadly fires both before that horrific incident and since exposed the fact that people were working in lethal conditions for poor pay in order for us to enjoy throwaway fashion. If you want to know more, check out Lucy Siegle's book *To Die For*. There are other considerations alongside the exploitation of workers:

➜ Producing cotton uses 22.5 per cent of the world's insecticides and 10 per cent of the world's pesticides, as well as vast quantities of water.

← Chemicals used to treat textiles are big pollutants.

➜ Landfill is being clogged by disposable fashion.

← Animal welfare standards are compromised by high demand for fashionable fabrics like angora (from rabbits) or cashmere (from goats).

There has been a response. The 2015 Modern Slavery Act means that all companies with a turnover of more than £36 million that operate in the UK have to at least question whether there's any suspicion of either slavery or human trafficking in their supply chains. And the situation is complicated, as the manufacturing industry in Asia offers steady employment that can lift people out of poverty, so there's no question of consigning it to history just yet. One way of salving your conscience is constructing a cost-per-wear equation. That means you estimate the value of an item based on how much you wear it. So don't fall for an outfit with threads that are already unravelling that you will only wear once.

Instead look towards the costly item that you know in your heart you will always adore. It's an antidote to throwaway fashion, with the underlying message 'buy less, buy better'.

On which point, clothes are, like other goods and services, subject to the Consumers Rights Act 2015 (see p. 10). They must be SQUAD Fit for Life, and all the in-store policies in the world can't change that. I'd say I've had most of my arguments in shops on this point, mainly before the advent of smart phones, which give you a bit of a fait accompli with stubborn salespeople. 'Google it!'

BOOM!

Matt Stat

Research carried out in 2018 showed that Britons, on average, wear only 27 per cent of their wardrobe in a calendar year. I regularly wear my Ikea wardrobe out and find it ill-fitting, heavy and awkward.

Matt Nav

I buy loads of clothes second-hand. I know, you're surprised, right? Because I'm, like, a massive fashion icon. Why? Well, I don't like new things, generally. Old threads cost a fraction of new stuff and have more character, and when I'm done I'm happy to pass them on again for someone else to use. I do draw the line at undies and socks. What really upsets me is the huge industry that's emerged buying old clothes for cash, usually by weight. They're usually being transported to Eastern Europe to be sold on and reused, which is great, but you can't help thinking they're wondering over in Kiev why we need so many. Do watch out for mobile charity collections of clothes, which can be a scammy front for the same sort of commercial business. Make sure you see ID before handing anything over.

WHITE GOODS

The clichés all work here. Buy cheap, buy twice. Buy in haste, repent at leisure, and so on. Generally, you get what you pay for. Whatever your budget, to work out the value of your machine it's worth establishing a predicted lifespan for your washing machine, drier, dishwasher or vacuum, and spreading the up-front cost over those years. Sadly, the truth is that that lifespan has diminished over the last few decades, with whispers of 'built-in-redundancy' getting louder all the time. Add to this the technological advances that have been made, particularly with TVs (smart goods, etc.), and it's tempting to see these products as disposable, when our parents' expectation would be that they should last a lifetime.

Most white goods can be loosely grouped into three price categories: budget, mid-range and top end. What you might not know at first glance is that many of the machines that you're looking at will come from the same manufacturing group or even the same factory. For example, the Electrolux group includes AEG and Zanussi, while Bosch, Siemens and Neff all stand under the BSH umbrella, and Hoover and Baumatic cuddle up with Candy. Whirlpool now takes in Hotpoint and Indesit as well as Maytag.

> *A longer warranty, say three years, is the sign of a manufacturer who is confident they won't have an expensive repair bill*

Part of the key here is to have a good long hard look at what happens if your machine goes wrong. A longer warranty, say three years, is the sign of a manufacturer who is confident they won't have an expensive repair bill, because their machine is bombproof. After-sales warranties are available, and are often pushed enthusiastically by a sales force with upselling targets. They're often third-party financial products backed by a company that doesn't have its reputation on the line like the manufacturer. The cost can be greater than a repair. I mean, maybe you can tell I'm not a fan. If you want to be mathematical about it, find out how much they cost, and stick the cash to one side for a rainy day. If you never use it... PARTY!

Let's go through some of the big white good categories:

Washing machines

Usage is key here, because you're going to want something that lasts. If your house resembles Widow Twankey's laundry then don't skimp. Go big drum for fewer loads, and as close to top end as you can afford. The average household usage for a washing machine is between 250 and 280 loads per year. A 6-kg drum will wash a single

> The average household usage for a washing machine is between 250 and 280 loads per year.

duvet, or five pairs of jeans and t-shirts. A 10-kg drum does a king-size duvet or ten tops and bottoms. Inside, all washing machines look a bit similar. Budget manufacturers can bump up their selling price by sticking in a bigger drum or increasing spin speed but it can be a false economy. Unless it's up to the task, that washing machine's heroic spinning action is going to drive you loopy when it starts dancing around the kitchen under its own steam. Once, not that long ago, great advice for washing machine buyers would be to avoid sealed tubs without access to the bearings, as these are tricky to repair. Now almost all models have sealed tubs, something that's accelerated the demand for washing machines in the UK. Effectively, if the bearings fail then the cost of repairs – running into several hundred pounds – usually compels people to buy a new machine. The cost of the bearings alone would be something in the order of £20. Did I mention built-in redundancy? It's worth finding out how long your manufacturer expects their machines to last – for any of the white goods in this chapter. Often they'll have mentioned it in press releases or reviews. What they admit constitutes a 'reasonable' life span could be a crucial factor if your washer breaks down outside warranty and you want to bring the CRA2015 into play (see p. 10). Remember: SQUAD Fit for Life!

Tumble driers

Most tumble driers fall into three plug-and-go categories: vented, condenser and heat pump. Vented driers are the cheapest to buy but you will need to find a way to pipe the hot moist air out of the room. You don't need that with condenser driers, although you will usually need to empty the tank in the bottom, which fills with water from the wet clothes, unless it's plumbed in. Make sure the tank is easy to access before deciding which model to buy. The same goes for heat pump models, which are more expensive than the rest but far less costly to run. And the energy saving can amount to more than £70 a year here, so they are definitely worth consideration. There are gas driers, which are cheaper still to operate but harder to find and have to be fitted by an engineer. Choose a drum size – between 3 kg and 9 kg – to match the number of people in your family, bearing in mind that they work better when they are full. For reference, a kg of clothes is usually a full outfit: top, trousers, undies and socks. It's a good idea to have a drier that's somewhere close to the capacity of your washing

> It's a good idea to have a drier that's somewhere close to the capacity of your washing machine so you don't have wet clothes hanging around.

machine so you don't have wet clothes hanging around waiting for their moment in the sun. Most now have a sensor that stops the tumbling action when washing is dry. The aim is to save time and electricity above a manual setting but it doesn't always work. If you need work clothes, it might be worth investing in one with above-basic settings, like anti-crease or iron dry, to make laundry aftercare easier.

Dishwashers

What you are looking for here is high cleaning power and low noise level. Choose a model that suits the size of your family. A standard sized model will accommodate some 150 items at a time. Slimline versions are 15 cm less in width (roughly 45cm) and can hold about 100 pieces. Options include things like adjustable racks, a timer, a sensor that works out how dirty the dishes are and some gadgetry that makes it wifi enabled. If looks count for you, there are integrated dishwashers that sit discreetly behind a kitchen cabinet door. But one of the most important figures is how much it costs to run. According to *Which?* the best full-sized dishwasher it found used a miserly half-litre of water during a cycle, compared to 1.8 litres in the least economical model. (That compares to an estimated 9 litres that would be used in hand washing.) Meanwhile, at £30 per annum, the cheapest model in electrical usage cost less than half to run against the greediest.

Fridge/freezers

> Ask yourself, could you not put a jug of water on a fridge shelf and buy an icemaker for a nearby work-surface?

Despite a whopping price tag, American-style fridges are bang on trend at the moment for those with huge kitchens that can accommodate the commodious budget-busting side-by-side freezer and refrigerator. Many people are starry eyed about its ability to dispense cold water and ice. But ask yourself, could you not put a jug of water on a fridge shelf and buy an icemaker for a nearby work-surface? And do you really need all that shelf space or will it get cluttered with food in various stages of decomposition? Some have alluring gadgets like 'vacation mode'. The clever money says you never, ever use it. What you should be looking for is robust door seals to keep the fridge chilly as well as its ability to rapidly cool food, for the purposes of good food hygiene. Yet to catch on in this country is the magical corner fridge – a TARDIS-like invention that makes use of that tricky space in the corner of your kitchen. There's a free business opportunity for someone. Fill your salad drawer!

Ovens

Ask yourself which fuel will power your oven and the answer will probably be immediately obvious, given your domestic circumstances. Electricity is the most common choice, gas ovens are getting rare and oil is only suitable for very few properties. Size is dictated by the layout of your kitchen, so that also limits your choice. If you're plumping for a double electric oven, have a good long hard look, and possibly take some advice about your electrics before you order. Not every kitchen electricity supply is up to the task of doing your turkey and roasties at the same time. Melty wiring and house fires can really take the edge off Christmas, let me tell you.

With those details sorted, take a look at some basics. Once again, door seals are key, as well as insulation, to keep the oven at the correct temperature. The other big factors to consider are how soon it hits the right temperature and how evenly that heat is spread around inside the oven. Do you want a fan oven for more even cooking at lower heat and general crispiness? Would you like your oven to super-heat and clean itself every so often? You need to research the answer to questions like these before heading into a showroom. But once there, see how easy it is to peer into the oven, make sure the shelves are plentiful and free-wheeling, and ask how much installation will cost so

> *Big factors to consider are how soon it hits the right temperature and how evenly that heat is spread around inside the oven.*

that doesn't come as a nasty shock. Peruse other aspects – like a self-cleaning oven surface, digital controls and a timer – at your leisure. There are common design flaws to watch for too. There have been numerous examples of handles becoming too hot to, well, handle with cheaper models. Go to the relevant websites to research reviews before making a final choice.

Hobs

Induction hobs are the latest, safest innovation on cooker tops. Somewhere beneath the glass there's a coil that, using magnetic induction, heats up the bottom of your pan when it's switched on. As if by magic, the ring doesn't stay hot if you accidentally leave it on, so the chances of being burned are vastly reduced, and it works fast, so saves money. Gas is now in danger of losing its top-of-the-tree position as the most versatile and cheapest option – although chefs still love it. Induction needs a big chunk of ferrous metal in the base of the pan to work. Stainless steel and iron pans work, while others have to be made specially. Test yours with a magnet and, if it sticks, they will work. If you've got a pacemaker, induction is not the choice for you unless you're actively trying to avoid cooking. The magnet can mess with your ticker while you're making chicken tikka.

Vacuum cleaners

Invented in 1860, the vacuum cleaner has come a long way. These days they come cordless, bagless, upright, smart – or none of the above. Upright vacuums are probably the best choice if you have plush carpets but beware cord length, which varies considerably between models and could limit your horizons. Compact vacuums are easier to tow around when it comes stairs and small corners. Watch out for the ongoing cost of branded bags that are needed to collect the debris – these are the hidden costs of a cheap vaccy. Rechargeable vacuums will have you skipping around the house, but not for long as there's a limit to their battery life, and you'll need to check you can buy a replacement battery when it eventually gives up. You won't need vacuum bags as the rubbish collects in a canister but it is considered more unhygienic to empty these compared to rival models with bags. You may well want the versatility of a cordless with the power of an upright. Immerse yourself in the exciting world of detachable heads, by all means, but keep it real. Ask yourself when you genuinely last needed to clean a ceiling fan.

> *Watch out for the ongoing cost of branded bags that are needed to collect the debris – these are the hidden costs of a cheap vaccy.*

Matt Nav

Every week some 60 house fires flare up after white goods combust. Whirlpool has been at the centre of the kitchen blaze scandal and in 2019 the company finally recalled 80,000 tumble driers and more than half a million washing machines. That extended across all the Whirlpool brands including Hotpoint, Indesit, Creda, Swan and Proline. To be honest, they've made a right Horlicks of the whole thing, failing to properly acknowledge the scale of the tumble drier problem, and then neglecting to put anyone in the UK permanently who could talk to all those customers. Whoever your manufacturer, there are some safety steps householders should take:

- Tumble drier fluff is one of the best firelighters in the world. Keep your filters clear at all times.

- Keep a domestic fire extinguisher in the kitchen.

- Don't overload sockets.

- Don't run dish washers, washing machines and tumble driers at night.

- Read the operating manual carefully to identify risks.

TV AND ENTERTAINMENT

What makes your TV smart? Well, it's not just the people who appear on it (insincere smile). It means it's connected to the internet for a start, which means it can stream entertainment services like Netflix, access on-demand television from BBC iPlayer and the like and even has a web browser with which you can look up other services. New televisions can be linked up to virtual assistants like Alexa who will change the channel for you if you ask it to. What will they think of next? So that's all clever stuff and that's why your furniture all points towards it. But it's also the reason that your telly on average now lasts just a few years before being replaced.

The industry keeps finding ways to upgrade – from CRT to plasma, LED, OLED. From HD to UHD to 4K to 8K, we're always being provided with reasons why what we have in our front rooms isn't quite up to scratch. Then comes the itch to move on, with a ruinous effect on our pockets and the environment. Size matters too: 65-inch sets now account for nearly 20 per cent of all tellies sold, possibly to people who haven't worked out that they could save their money and just sit a little bit closer. While recommendations vary across manufacturers, one standard is that you should sit at a distance of between 1.5 and 2.5 times the screen size. So if you were watching on a 50-inch screen your chair should be some 10 feet away from it.

I don't mean to sound like a luddite, but a TV, like so much tech now, isn't looking like the

> We're always being provided with reasons why what we have in our front rooms isn't quite up to scratch.

investment it once was, and the disposability of such a big chunk of machine is, frankly, a bit sickening. In any case, there are many ways to future-proof your telly. I've had the same one for 15 years, and thanks to the array of boxes you can dangle and dongle out of the back, you won't miss out on too much of the fun. You may not be able to use the full definition of the screen as it moves through the gears towards perfection, but hey, like flying first class, you'll never miss what you haven't had. A lot of the gimmicky stuff that gets loaded onto tellies doesn't last that long anyway – remember 3D TV? How much did that cost us? It's a matter of taste whether you think the different iterations of Plasma and LED are a huge improvement on older technology anyway. Personally, I think they can make classic films look cheap.

Anyway. Back down off my high horse, telly is actually great. Most homes get at least some of their telly via the internet these days, so if your broadband is not speedy enough your television picture will be splintered at best. It is possible to connect the broadband hub to the television by cable, to improve matters. Another thing to point out about smart tellies. They're a form of media loyalty card scheme, a bit like the ones the supermarkets operate (see p. 85). You probably didn't realise but when you agreed to the t's and c's of the television you agreed that they could suck up all the information in your television journeys. In a benign way, they might want to use that big data to curate a suggested viewing list. In a more sinister way, they could use it to target advertising at you, at home, in your armchair, all unawares. Comforting or creepy, your choice, but it _is_ your choice. It should be possible to enjoy smart televisions and disentangle yourself from tracking, without losing access to the relevant platforms. Check with your manual or the company that wrote it.

Matt Stat

2018 research in the US found that the average size of a TV set has more than doubled from 22 inches in 1997 to 48 inches two decades later.

SMART TECH AND ASSISTANTS

As I write, I'm listening to BBC Radio 3 on my female-characterised assistant. But is she listening to me? She's certainly multi-talented, with the ability to integrate with household functions like heating, lighting and telephones, in what's become known as the Internet of Things or IoT. This interconnection means that these devices – which are actually cloud-based technology expressed through a speaker – can join forces with your music apps to play special requests or give you an update on the news and weather, but also dim the lights, lock the doors and tell you when the washing machine cycle has ended. If you struggle with mobility or dexterity this must be a massive step forward. But for all of us, there are some red flags on the horizon.

Makers will tell you that the smart tech only springs into action when it hears its name. But critics have wondered if the speakers through which Alexa operates were a privacy concern as they could act as eavesdroppers. This seemed to be proved in 2018 when a couple discovered a conversation they'd had was recorded and sent to a random address in their contacts book. It's what happens when artificial intelligence gets too clever.

Amazon insisted the assistant woke up on command and interpreted words spoken during the conversation as commands.

How can the tech giants behind these devices use our data to sell us things from other people? Surely that's what the GDPR laws of 2018 were brought in to prevent? Well, Google say that while they use the info they have on us to bring opportunities to buy stuff to our attention, they never actually share our data with anyone. So they're playing within the rules, in a slightly creepy, all-encompassing and controlling way.

> *How can the tech giants behind these devices use our data to sell us things from other people?*

COMPUTERS

In one way or another, computers contain our heart and soul now. Lose them and that vital information about our innermost workings is soon in the hands of crooks. But security is the watchword and it is in our hands:

→ Make sure automatic updates linked to operating systems are downloaded.

← Use antivirus and anti-malware programmes to help keep would-be invaders at bay.

→ Look for the wireless or 'WLAN' settings on your router and set them to the latest WPA2 standard. Make sure your router's firewall is up to date too.

← Make better passwords. The days when we could use our middle names followed by 1234 are gone. You can strengthen passwords by using upper and lower case letters, numbers and special keyboard characters like % and *. If you are fearful about forgetting them sort yourself out a password manager that will generate and record passwords for you, so you can have plenty of them with having a headache.

→ Don't click on suspicious email links (see p. 51).

← Be wary about downloading new software.

→ Don't trust the pop-ups that tell you your current protection is out of date and that you must the link click now. The notification appears garish, flashing and a bit threatening. But once again it's OOTBNFY.

BEDS AND MATTRESSES

From the technically challenging to the most basic and essential. We spend hours stretched out in bed – on average 2,548 in the year – so you want to get your mattress right. The good news is that the best may not necessarily be the most expensive, and there are plenty of newcomers trying to stir up the mattress market. One thing matters: trying the thing out before you commit. It's personal, and everyone who's using the mattress should have some say. Don't lie down in your coat for five seconds, leap up out of embarrassment and do the deal. That way lie restless nights and arguments.

Sizes differ, even within the single, queen, double, king and super-king definitions. Know your bedstead dimensions before you start looking. Switching sizes can be expensive, as you'll be swapping all your bedding too. Don't do what we did and sleep for 20 years under a duvet that's too small for the bed. Tug-of-war every single night. Idiots.

There are four types of mattress out there, two of which feature metal coils. The pocket-sprung mattress

> *The good news is that the best may not necessarily be the most expensive.*

has each one snug in a compartment of its own, compared to the open-sprung mattress, with its coils lying in a sheet. In broad terms, pocket-sprung mattresses are supportive and are likely to be made with natural materials so get less sweaty than some of the alternatives. Open-sprung mattresses are cheaper to make but offer less support. For both it's the number of coils, the thickness of the wire and their tension that make all the difference. Then there are memory foam mattresses, which mould to the body's shape and stay warm, and finally the durable foam or latex type – best for allergies as they are most resistant to house mites. Some mattresses have elements of more than one type. For example, a sprung mattress could have a memory foam top.

If you've only ever bought a mattress from a shop before, it's worth having a long hard look at the online mattress sellers, even if it's just for the joy of taking it out of its vacuum-packed parcel and watching it blossom into spongey wonderfulness. These are typically competitively priced, top many consumer test lists, and should give you a long trial period before you have to commit. I actually have no idea how they do it, but they do, and if it means a good sleep for us all, I'm in.

Don't make the mistake of thinking a hard mattress will be a tonic for your aching back. The most comfortable will be the one that supports your spine so your body stays the same shape as it would if you were upright. Sweet dreams!

FURNITURE

After your bed, it's likely that the next place you spend the most time is your sofa, settee, couch, futon, daybed or Davenport. Comfort and durability are our watchwords here, and it's upstairs for comfort, downstairs for durability. If the frame is made of softwood, like pine, it's likely to be less durable, and should be at the cheaper end of the range. Hardwood is harder-working.

To test the frame strength, lift one front corner of the sofa so the leg is about six inches off the floor. By now the other front leg should be rising too. If it's not, the frame already has too much flexibility in it and won't last the marathon of a thousand evenings in, as all its joints will go wobbly. With wooden frames there should be evidence of dowels, wooden corner blocks or even metal screws and brackets, and it is these that illustrate durability. The legs should be integral to the frame. Avoid anything that's held together by staples, nails and glue alone.

> To test the frame strength, lift one front corner of the sofa so the leg is about six inches off the floor.

In the upholstery there are likely to be springs, with hand-tied springs the most sought after. Look for ones that are close together and firm to the touch. Sofas without springs are long-term uncomfortable alternatives. Usually, it's the cushions that are the big selling point. The textile should be tough enough to withstand years of wear. Cotton, linen, wool, microfibres and leather are usually strong contenders, all of which can be treated to resist stains. A blend of natural and synthetic fibres is likely to quickly show its age. Textured fabric always sits better than an entirely smooth material. Like a mattress, spend proper time on your prospective sofa before you buy it. High-backed seats look more at home in rooms with high ceilings while low-slung backs give an illusion of space. You also need to make sure it isn't six inches too wide for the lounge door. There is a complex set of calculations to work out if a sofa fits through an opening. Make sure whoever's selling it to you can help with this, and if it's looking close, make sure they are prepared to take the thing back.

Matt Stat

3 in 10 Brits have sent furniture to the landfill which could have been recycled (2018).

WAYS OF PAYING

If you've got cash saved up, then you're sorted. For most of us though, big-ticket items will require some sort of credit. Of course, I'm going to tell you to have a long hard look at paying using a credit card, for the invaluable Section 75 protection that comes with it (see p. 23). You will have to pay it off at the end of the month to avoid painful APR though. This is one area where stores know enough to offer 0 per cent interest-free credit. Fabulous, but nothing comes for nothing, and it's unlikely this will accompany any kind of discount. Also, putting payments off 'til another day feels good until that day comes. Debt is debt, even without interest payments.

In-store credit cards

Until 2011 in-store credit cards were a great option when it came to costly purchases because the stores usually offered a juicy enticement to take one out. That's no longer happening and store cards tend to have a higher rate of interest than other commercial rivals. Beware establishment fees, which might even be followed by monthly fees. If so, know that there's always a better deal out there than that. **Always check the percentage rates and make sure payments are affordable.**

Hire purchase

This is a type of loan but you don't own the item you've bought until the last repayment is made. It means you can't do anything with the purchased item – like sell it – as it's not yours, and it could be taken back if you falter on payments. Having said that, you can end the agreement and return the goods by choice.

0 per cent finance cards

Here's a credit card that's charging 0 per cent on the money it's forwarding for your use. That's great news – but use the card wisely. You still have to pay the debt down by a set amount each month and your aim should be to pay off the debt entirely while credit remains free. That means when normal charges kick in – the card company will tell you when – you are all paid up already. Some people with poor credit ratings struggle to get the best of these deals. **Always check final percentage rates.**

Buy now, pay later

Some stores offer a buy now, pay later scheme (BNPL), which helps if you have been landed with an unexpected cost, like a washing machine breakdown. It's wrapped in a coat of flexibility but once again, it only makes financial sense if you ensure you pay off the amount during the interest-free period set down in the agreement. It could be costly if you don't. Some outlets offer you the chance to have multiple BNPL schemes running at the same time. Of course they do. They are rubbing their hands together, waiting for the day you have to start paying interest on them all. **Always check the percentage rates.**

Catalogue credit

Many catalogues offer people the chance to buy now, pay later with dedicated accounts. They say it gives you a great chance to spread the cost of shopping. I'd say this way of doing things comes from another age, before Primark, fast fashion and the way people shop now. The reality is that it's definitely going to cost you more than if you'd paid in cash. If you miss a payment the cost will spiral, sooooo … **always check the percentage rates.**

SHOPPING ONLINE

I spent most of my teenage years hanging around shopping centres, waiting for friends I couldn't locate because mobile phones hadn't been invented. But the simple truth is that increasingly that's not how we're buying things these days. After the COVID-19 lockdown, that's only likely to increase.

There are advantages to internet shopping that the high street cannot match. Parking, carrying stuff, crowds, rain and ignorance – all of these disappear when you're shopping online. Not to mention the ability to search for the very best price in an almost risk-free environment, thanks to the CCR 2013 (see p. 19), which allow us to return things and get a refund when we buy at a distance.

> *Parking, carrying stuff, crowds, rain and ignorance – all of these disappear when you're shopping online*

There are drawbacks, though, and it's worth being aware of them, as we input our name, address, delivery address, etc., and squint to see which of the squares does contain traffic lights. Every purchase, or even enquiry, has the potential to let advertisers into your digital life. As with digital assistants (see p. 20) it's no

Every purchase, or even enquiry, has the potential to let advertisers into your digital life.

coincidence that any show of interest for waterproof hats will result in endless email and pop-up adverts offering you ways to keep your head dry. Shut down pop-ups on your browser. Don't click on them unless you want to wreak a horrible revenge on the real owner of the computer.

We deal with online safety loads in the previous chapter on Scams (see p. 28). But e-commerce is a perpetual target for scammers and as an online shopper you need to know the site you are using is safe. Here are five things to look for:

→ In the address line, instead of http, seek out https as the s stands for secure. It indicates the first step towards internet safety has been taken.

← Better still, the address line will be picked out in green and there will be a symbol indicating further security measures are in place, probably in the form of a closed padlock. That guarantees your information will be encrypted en route to the sales site.

→ Make sure there is a physical address on the website for the vendor and be suspicious if there's not.

← Look out for a returns policy – and read it. If there isn't one, it's a bad sign. Yes, there's the law, but they should go further.

→ Then search for a privacy policy. Don't forget, rogue websites will pirate not only your credit card details but also your data.

PUBLIC WIFI

You're out shopping, in an actual shop. But you need to catch up on your email, maybe even make a couple of payments. Your mobile connection flicks between 'E' and 3G. No good.

But hold on! This cafe offers a free wifi service! No password or anything! Let's hook up and get this done!

Please don't. Public wifi is a room where everyone can see what you're doing, on a big screen over your head. The things you're planning to do can give a scammer on the next table a good look at your bank details, and the email password that controls your accounts.

There are two types of public wifi, secure and unsecure. While there's usually some registration involved with the first, neither should have sight of your credit card or banking details. Your details won't be encrypted and they could be harvested by criminals. There are other ways of making yourself safe from internet exploitation too:

➜ Never send or receive personal information using public wifi.

← If you use public wifi, make sure you log out when you've finished so you are not walking around buzzing with connectivity.

Matt Nav

The Consumer Contracts Regulations 2013 (see p. 19) aren't just for Christmas. You've got the same rights in December and early January as at other times, although the best online retailers will offer terms and conditions which put tinsel and baubles on these.

One awful practice I've been on the end of is online traders who accept orders before they have the stock in hand. This is typical for 'hot' Christmas products, which the distributor promises to supply to the retailer before the 25th, but which may not make it to you by then – a fact you aren't told when you hand over your money. I dislike this practice so much I've invented a term for it: empty sledging. You've sent your letter to Santa, he's checked that you're not on the naughty list (your payment has cleared) but the goods weren't there to be sold and aren't physically on their way to you. Get an instant refund, as is your right under the CCR 2013, and spend the money with someone who isn't making stuff up. It's rude, Rudolph!

➡ For preference use a big name 'hot spot' which may have more security measures in place.

⬅ Turn off your Bluetooth when you are on the move. It's another route in to your private data. In case you forget, make sure your phone will only link to known paired devices.

➡ If you plan to do this lot for business, perhaps, use a secure Virtual Private Network or VPN.

⬅ Don't leave your smartphone, tablet or computer unattended.

➡ When you are using your device, be sure no-one is monitoring your usage by looking at it, or 'shoulder surfing' as it's known.

AUCTION SITES AND ONLINE MARKETPLACES

Auction sites and online marketplaces (think Amazon Marketplace) can feel a bit Wild-Westy, what with people starting up businesses and selling stuff to people they've never met. But they're not so wild that they're outside of UK law, namely the CCR 2013. After all, the Distance Selling Regulations from which the CCR regenerated were designed for exactly this type of purchase.

However, it's important to make a distinction between transactions between individuals and ones between businesses. If you're buying a pair of skis from some bloke who can't ski any more because he just broke his leg in two places (Val d'Isère and Kitzbuhel) then he doesn't have to offer you a refund if you're not happy. If, however, the same guy advertises as 'Second-Hand Ski Village', has 12 pairs up for sale and has sold 100 others, he's a business and the CCR 2013 apply. You don't like? Reject within a fortnight and you get a refund.

In addition, auction sites like eBay and marketplace arrangements will have their own rules set up for purchasers and sellers. They offer protection against purchases going sour through misdescription or failure to deliver. IMPORTANT BIT NOW!

These usually rely on the purchase going through the correct channel – i.e. through a fully-fledged eBay transaction, which means that eBay get their fees from the seller. Many scams rely on redirecting buyers away from the official purchase mechanism to avoid both the fees and the oversight. Be wary of any seller (or buyer, if you're selling) who wants a personal email or an alternative way of paying. You won't get any help if it goes wrong.

> Be wary of any seller (or buyer, if you're selling) who wants a personal email or an alternative way of paying.

Check the delivery method before buying to see if there's a cost implication. After all, it might be a collections policy rather than delivery. Scan the reviews to get an insight about the trader's history.

When you are buying from Europe, the consumer protection laws will be similar FOR NOW, although they may not be a mirror image of ours. However, there is the EU online dispute resolution service, which could help. FOR NOW.

Fakes are rife online. These fake items look genuine, although an absurdly low price for a high-end item is a big clue. But while cheapness is a red flag, it doesn't follow that a price close to the standard means you're safe. Fakes come with hidden hazards: fake cosmetics can be toxic; alcohol might contain additives that are poisonous and even lethal; toys could go under the health and safety radar and have choking hazards; electrical goods might be a fire risk; and clothes might also be unexpectedly flammable.

Look out for badly copied brand names and a lack of logo. The item may well not have the same distinguishing features as an original so examine the product description carefully. If in doubt, it's better to buy from a reputable retailer. Particularly in the case of big purchases, look for where there's likely to be a damaging loss of reputation if things go wrong. You'll probably find yourself opting for the names you know and trust.

It's stone-cold illegal to sell counterfeit goods. If you suspect you've bought a counterfeit item, report it first to the seller, in case they are not aware, and then to the site used by them. After that, put in a call to your local trading standards office. They may be able to shut down that channel, and stop others from losing out. You may be happy to have a handbag that looks iconic but came at a fraction of the proper cost. However, that desirable accessory has probably been made by forced labour, with the profits going into international organised crime. Oh! And they now have your credit card details.

chapter
four

Banking and Money

Banks aren't what they used to be, and that's both a blessing and a curse. For a start, a third of all bank branches have closed since 2015, mostly from the big four banks. OK, online banking means that most of us don't need to stand in queues waiting for our turn with the pen on the chain, but that's assuming you have access to the internet, or a smart phone.

Increasingly, the banking system looks like it's catering for those who already have access to plenty of money, and it's much less available to anyone who struggles with, or doesn't have access to tech. For those who do, however, the choice has never been wider, with a bunch of challenger banks – some online only – stepping in to make things, they say, easier.

The worlds of credit and debt have changed beyond recognition too. As a country we now have more personal debt than at any time in history – currently a whopping £1,400 per person. Rather than sourcing this from and managing it face to face with our friendly bank manager like our parents and grandparents might have done, we are now getting credit from new and exciting sources, often without any personal contact or assessment of whether it can be paid back. We've seen that lenders don't always have the best interests of their customers at heart, and the interest they charge makes your eyes water.

Overseeing all of this loosening up is the credit score system, a means of monitoring your reliability at paying back the credit you've taken. Your credit score can make the difference between fulfilling your dreams and facing hardship, and yet the process is still cloaked in a degree of mystery.

Add to this the prevalence of scams designed to rip that money out of your account, and it's never been a better time to grasp the basics of your bank balance and start making it work for you! Bowler hats and brollies at the ready! Let's bank!

As a country we now have more personal debt than at any time in history.

CHOOSING A BANK

You need a bank. You do. If you're going to be paid wages, own or rent a home, receive benefits or any of the other things that make up modern life, you need one. I'll be honest, if you're reading this and planning to live in the woods in a home you've built yourself from what you find around you, to clothe and feed yourself and your dependants using the products of your own labour, then I salute you. But... how and why did you buy this book?

The rest of us need a bank, at the very least a current account that stops us from hiding cash under the mattress. You'll be lucky if you get any interest at all on this account. It's definitely more important to make sure it suits you and you won't be charged huge fees for other bits and bobs without a good reason.

There are a few variations on a current account:

Fee-free

This is typically for anyone who has had money troubles in the past – a poor credit record or county court judgements. Basically, the banks are putting stabiliser wheels on your account for a bit until your finances are less wobbly. It protects you from crashing and burning by running up an overdraft and incurring the fees attached, and it protects them from, well, the same thing. You can receive your wages, pay direct debits and standing orders, and use a debit card as long you're in the black. It's a great way to build up confidence and your credit score. If everything goes OK there's a good chance they'll upgrade to a...

Standard current account

... with all the bells and whistles. You'll have an option to go overdrawn, but with the usual (and sometimes unexpectedly high) interest and fees attached. There's usually a big difference in the charges for an authorised and an unauthorised overdraft. Forget to speak to your bank and they'll make you pay, the little stinkers. But then if you took money out of my pocket without asking, I'd probably be a bit peeved too. The best way to prevent this is by making sure you set up a phone SMS alert to let you know when you're getting close to zero. When it pings, get in touch with the bank and let them know you'll be spending a little time in the red. It could save you a ton.

Offset account

Current accounts can be linked to a mortgage, giving customers the chance to offset whatever they've got against the outstanding sum to be repaid. This is magic – reducing payments or racking up a handy pot for use later. It's a great way to earn virtual interest on current accounts when there isn't really any being offered, because not paying the 2.5 per cent you would be on that amount is the same as receiving 2.5 per cent interest, and you'll be doing well to find that anywhere. The other massive plus is that unlike interest on savings, offset amounts don't attract taxation. Bonus!

Packaged account

Honestly, I'm not sure how they do these. For a monthly fee, typically about £15/month, you'll get a bundle of other financial products sellotaped on to your account. These are often things you might buy anyway, like global travel insurance, vehicle breakdown cover and mobile phone insurance. Now if you do your sums, a family of four or more could never get those bits and bobs for £200. Phone insurance alone could be that much. Before you switch though, best make sure they suit you. You won't be counting the pennies if your partner is stuck on the hard shoulder and they're not part of the breakdown deal.

Jam-jar account

This is more a way to organise your current account, allowing you to set up different pots of money. Say you're self-employed and you need to stick a bit away for the tax man, or you're saving for a holiday. Here's a way to make sure it doesn't get frittered away on frivolous things like food and shoes for the kids. I'm reliably informed that the bank actually uses old jam jars for this purpose, which makes the money a little sticky when you come to use it.

IS MY MONEY SAFE?

Well, I'll say it probably is, at least if the bank goes kaput. There are protections in place if your money is in an institution regulated by the Financial Conduct Authority (FCA), through a thing called the Financial Services Compensation Scheme (FSCS).

The magic number is £85,000. Anything you've got in a bank account, pension scheme, mortgage and a couple of other product types, is protected up to this amount in case the institution in question does a dying swan. This is not a theoretical exercise. During the financial crisis at the end of the noughties, the FSCS paid out a staggering £26 billion to customers when the City took a series of cold showers. If you've got more than that, you may want to spread it around a bit across other banks and building societies, you know, just in case.

Scam Protection

Watch your backs! When it comes to scams, the approach from the banks isn't anywhere near as organised or unified. In fact they've had a pretty miserable record of protecting their customers from being scammed, and on *Watchdog* we have shown that they're really reluctant to put things right when they fail to do so. The sums involved can be huge.

Matt Nav

RBS customer Charlotte Higman had more than £4,000 stolen from her account by a fraudster who fooled the bank's telephone banking systems. RBS call logs show a warning of 'potential account takeover' and the caller failing the bank's own voice recognition checks, but despite this, Charlotte's fraud claim was rejected, as was her complaint to the Financial Ombudsman Service, and it was only after *Watchdog* contacted RBS that it refunded Charlotte's money.

Funny (not funny) how a call from us can make two separate organisations change their minds. Maybe they should have a sign over their desks: 'How would I behave if I knew *Watchdog* was watching?'

Many banks have realised that scams are growing in number and sophistication (see p. 51 for a flavour of a few banking scams doing the rounds). They realise that their systems have to be up to the job, or their customers are going to be easy prey, and then they'll lose their savings and switch banks. As a result they've signed up to an agreement which states that if no blame can be ascribed to customers, they should be compensated for their loss. There are a couple of problems here:

➡ It's a voluntary code. Loads of banks haven't signed up. If yours hasn't, ask yourself (and them) why.

← The funding arrangement for this code ran out in December 2019. At the time of writing, there isn't a replacement. This code is, therefore, toast.

As a result, it looks like we're back in the gloomy old days of banks making up their own minds about who's to blame. Typically, they do this using the phrase 'gross negligence' as a decider. But are you grossly negligent if some dodgepot calls you displaying your bank's own telephone number and persuades you to make a transfer? It's a rhetorical question. A friend of mine lost £40,000 this way, and his bank said it was his fault, until he pulled out every stop and dug in for the long haul.

Victory was his, my friends. But it might not be yours.

OOTBNFY!

Matt Stat

It's bank fraud boom time! £616 million went missing from UK banks in the first six months of 2019 because of fraud. £207 million went through bank transfer scams: number spoofing, phishing and the like. That figure is 40 per cent up on the first half of 2018. Fill your boots, dodgepots! Everyone else, look alive.

SAVINGS

Wow! Interest rates are, as they say, historically low, and have been for a good decade now. Fab if you're a borrower, not so great if you've got spare cash. When things are like this, the very best thing you can do with your money is pay off your debts. Doing that will always get you better (virtual) interest than a savings account, because of the way savings and borrowing rates typically straddle the Bank of England rate. Borrowers pay more, savers get less, and paying off a debt that's costing 8 per cent APR is better than sticking the same money in an account that makes 1 per cent. But if you're completely debt free and still need to stick some away somewhere protected by the FSCS £85,000 threshold, there are a few options.

ISAs: Individual Savings Accounts

There are four types of ISAs, which will use your money in different ways to earn interest. They're offered by loads of different lenders, at different interest rates. The big draw of an ISA, compared to a traditional savings account, is that whatever you earn as interest comes to you tax-free. You'll have to pay tax on the money when you initially earn it, of course. It's not a total Seychelles-style tax dodge.

The four types are:

→ Cash ISAs: You put cash in, you take cash out. The bank, building society or investment company sticks it into something profitable in the meantime and pays you interest. You can get at it within 15 days but you might lose a bit of the interest on it.

← Stocks and Shares ISAs: Similar deal, but your money is going into, er, well, you get it. They can only be stocks and shares of a few certain types. You can get at your money within a month, but the interest penalties still apply.

→ Lifetime ISAs: Designed to help with house buying or retirement. You get an extra 25 per cent bonus on anything you save up to £4,000. Don't bother trying to take one out if you're over 40, people. Our time has gone. You also can't contribute any more after 50. You can get money out when you buy a home up to £450,000 with a mortgage, or when you're 60. Funny one really, one product for two very different stages of life.

← Innovative Finance ISA: Brought in in 2016, this one is a newborn ISA that hasn't really learned to walk. It's designed to help you invest in peer-to-peer lending schemes and other growing financial structures, of which very few have been approved. It's riskier than most investments, and not protected by the FSCS. If that's something you're interested in, then you probably already know more than I do, so I won't waste your time. Good luck!

Because they're designed for individuals, not big business trying to dodge tax, there is a limit to how much you can stick into ISAs every tax year, running April to March. It's £20,000 into either Cash, Stocks and Shares or Innovative Finance, or a mix of the three. There's a separate limit of £4,000 for Lifetime ISAs.

BORROWING

For my dad's generation, and the one that came before him, debt was a dirty word. But used responsibly, credit, and therefore debt, aren't in themselves bad things. Quite the opposite, they can be positively liberating. Without credit, most of us would never own our own homes, or would spend lifetimes saving up for things whose use we could enjoy in the here and now. It is a sad reality, though, that because of the way the people who lend to us assess risk, borrowing is usually more expensive for those who need it the most. Even if you don't own a yacht, you can make the most of what you've got to make yourself as attractive as possible to lenders.

> Without credit, most of us would never own our own homes, or would spend lifetimes saving up for things.

Credit scoring

On first appearances, credit scoring looks appealingly
sporty. A bit like golf, perhaps. After all, you're trying
to hit a perfect number like a pro, to win all the things
that credit can get you. Indeed, the big credit scoring
companies who hold your financial lives in the palms
of their hands will give you an idea of the ranges of
score you need to be considered 'Good', 'Very Good' or
'Exceptional'. It's a system from which none of us can opt
out. They base these judgements on:

→ Current levels of debt

← How long you've had your bank accounts, credit cards,
loans, etc.

→ How often you've applied, and for how much credit

← Whether you pay on time

→ How much credit you have available compared to how
much you're using

← Bumps in the road like County Court Judgements
(CCJs) or Individual Voluntary Arrangements (IVA) to
pay back debts

→ Whether you're on the electoral roll

And from this you'll get a score between 0 (Latin American
dictator with a thing for tanks and Rolexes) and 999

(Richard Branson's mate who lends him money). How firms then use this information is to look at the specifics of their credit product and see how your score matches what they're trying to offer, and the sort of interest rates you'll get. It's all based on risk: if they see a chance, based on your score and history, that you'll fail to pay back credit, then they're either going to say a flat 'no' or make sure that their reward, in the form of interest payments, makes up for the risk they're taking. Even if you're not in the market for new lines of credit, a credit report can be a good tool for taking the temperature of your financial health and behaviours, and may well flag up any problems on the horizon. It's always worth checking for inconsistencies and mistakes. They happen, and can be corrected. There are also some concrete steps you can take to getting your credit score up there with Lord Sugar's.

→ Get a credit card. Use it and pay it off every month, by direct debit it you're forgetful like me. This will also give you a way to get Section 75 protection on what you buy (see p. 23).

← Get on the electoral roll. A lot of people worry this gives away their identity and address, but at the very least, opt out of the 'open' register (available to everyone) and stick to the 'full register' which lenders use to check you out. Registering anonymously means you're off both, but you have to show a reason why you need to do so, like being a spy or the person who invented Crazy Frog.

➡ Pay everyone on time, stay out of court and be nice to animals. Remember, your score is not based on whether you need credit or not. Most people do at some point. It's based on showing that you can be trusted to pay it back. Flexing your credit muscle when you don't need it means it will be ready for when you do.

There are only a few credit rating agencies: Experian, Equifax and TransUnion. I don't think it's unfair to say that Experian has traditionally been more open than the others about how it compiles your score. It's still a bit of a dark art, though. The credit providers won't tell you how they judge your trustworthiness when you apply, and sometimes the system really doesn't seem to make sense. If credit scoring is a game of golf, then it's one where you have no map of the course, no idea how far away the hole is or in which direction it lies. The credit scoring companies, meanwhile, are that guy who's standing just behind you, criticising your swing.

Matt Stat

The average total household debt in the UK is around £15,400 (2019).

PENSIONS

There are three types of pension, all designed to provide for you later in life, and all working in different ways.

State pension

As long as you've paid your National Insurance for ten qualifying years or more (not necessarily consecutive years), you'll get a state pension of some sort. If you've worked and paid NI for 30 years, you'll get the full amount: as I write, £168.60 per week. This sum is 'triple locked' to increase every year against the highest of three different measures: average earnings, the cost of living or 2.5 per cent. This means pensions will always go up, never down. If you don't know how much NI you've paid over the years you can check by getting a statement at https://www.gov.uk/check-state-pension. It's best to do this sooner rather than later. You can make voluntary payments before retirement to get yourself over the line, but it's probably worth sitting down and working out whether it's worth it. As with most pension chat, this is a fun discussion involving establishing a rough guesstimate of when you think you're going to die. Look out for that as an ongoing theme, pension fans!

Matt Nav

There have been a load of changes to the state pension in the past few years. One of the main ones is an attempt to cut the overall pension bill by pushing back and equalising the retirement age at which you can start claiming your pension. One of the most controversial things the government did was to take women's retirement age to 65, from where it will increase in line with men's, over the next couple of decades, to 68. All very fair and equal, except this change took place in the blink of an eye, meaning 3.8 million women born in the 1950s who were looking forward to collecting their pension suddenly faced up to six years' wait – with just a year's notice to sort out their finances. Many of them don't have the workplace or private pensions that their male counterparts had, and at a time when employment opportunities can be limited, they are struggling to keep the wolf from the door.

Workplace pensions

The ultimate perk for loyalty: years behind a desk are rewarded with guaranteed comfort when you reach retirement. Workplace pensions are marvellous for a couple of reasons. Firstly, your contributions are deducted automatically from your salary. You'll hardly notice them going out. Secondly, they're usually matched by contributions from your employer, so you double your money. Thirdly, you can get tax relief on the payments if your employer takes them out before tax. Your employer has to provide a pension scheme for you if you're over 22 and you earn more than £10,000 a year in the UK. You can opt out of paying in, and your employer can't force, persuade or encourage you to do so.

When it comes to paying out, your workplace pension takes a couple of different forms. **Defined contribution** schemes mean you'll pay in a certain amount, matched by your employer and tax relief from the government combined. It's a team effort, but what you receive will be defined by how much you've paid in and how it's invested. Your pot can go up or down, and a lot depends on how you decide to take your money, which can be taxed. **Defined benefit** (often called final

> *Your employer has to provide a pension scheme for you if you're over 22 and you earn more than £10,000 a year in the UK.*

salary) pensions are becoming as rare as giant pandas, because they pay a guaranteed sum for life at retirement. No depressing chats about having too much life left at the end of your pension. Just budget and plan, budget and plan. Firms don't like offering these because, quite frankly, people are living far too long these days. If you can find one, cling on to it and don't let it go.

Private (or personal) pensions

For the humble self-employed person, without a mothership company to take them in, the private pension is the only way to supplement whatever you're getting from the state. Compared to a workplace pension with its double bubble employer contributions, these are, honestly, slightly depressing affairs, usually because of the level of fees charged by even the big providers, which can easily whittle down your pot to a much skinnier sum. It's still subject to the whims of the market, and that means, as the voiceover man says, your investment can go up AND down. You do get tax relief on your contributions, which is something, and there's a lot of flexibility about how much you can invest, and where that investment goes: shares, property, cash or bonds.

I've kept this bit short on purpose because the world of pensions requires proper, detailed advice that matches your circumstances, and probably needs the best part of a book all to itself. I wouldn't want you to think otherwise.

chapter five

Phones (and Phoneys), Broadband and a Little Bit of TV

My memories of being a teenager are dominated by episodes of holding my nose in ammonium-filled telephone boxes, jamming ten pence pieces into slots in a desperate effort to find out where all my friends had gone. Now? I paid for my lunch with a watch which has just told me that Prince Harry is moving to Canada.

> I paid for my lunch with a watch which has just told me that Prince Harry is moving to Canada.

It's fair to say that things in the world of telephony have moved on a bit in the last ten years (OK, thirty-odd). Portable devices have changed from novelty pocket bricks to near-essentials, providing us with an umbilical link to our professional and business lives. For many of us, being without one is unthinkable, and for a few, not having the latest model is social suicide. Of course there is a much bigger question that people are asking about the real cost of our obsession with technology, and whether we really need to upgrade our devices as often as we do, but as the butterfly collector said, let's just put a pin in that for now and move on. If we accept we have to have phones and keep them up to date, let's make sure we're getting the best deal possible.

The terrific news is that along with the hardware and software space race, there is a fiercely competitive market on the high street and online to get you on the line. The other side of this coin is the bad news though: this market is as competitive as the final rounds of Strictly, and grinning salespeople are prepared to do almost anything to sign you up, including stretching the truth and their professional ethics wafer-thin. It's happened to me! Cheeky sods.

HOW TO CHOOSE A MOBILE PHONE

Visit an actual phone shop with actual people in it and you could be forgiven for being confused. You'll be confronted by names and terms that sound, in some cases, literally alien. Then you'll be asked to consider a commitment over a number of months which requires a lot of high-speed mental arithmetic. However it's broken down, chances are you're about to commit to parting with considerable wedge, so let's slow it down and get back to basics. Many of the choices you're going to make are binary, and relatively straightforward.

iPhone vs Android

What you are really talking about here is different operating systems: the software inside the phone. It's important to know that while many manufacturers (Samsung, Huawei, Motorola, Sony) make Android phones, only Apple make the kit that runs theirs. It's called iOS. If you have other Apple products then you will be used to the way iOS functions so it's probably your favourite, and it means that all your tech bits and bobs will be able to talk to each other more easily (see Charlie below). Equally, if you already own an Android tablet, that could be the way forward. Both systems are versatile and offer loads of applications (apps), but don't expect them to talk to each other. That's why people are usually one or the other, and some are fiercely brand-loyal and proud, which is fine, I suppose, if you don't have other hobbies or any real friends.

Let's think about what you need your phone for. If your needs are pretty straightforward, you can save a load of money by swerving features you'll never use.

Matt Nav

I'm lucky that I do have one or two real friends. I'm even luckier because one of them is someone I'll call Charlie. He's the manager of a branch of a major phone shop and sees it all happening in front of his eyes. I asked him to tell me all the things that people don't know when they buy phones. For one, he said the line between Apple and Android is getting blurred. More people are using apps like WhatsApp, which work on both systems, so if you change it's not so painful. Android have even developed Google Duo, an app that helps you stay in touch with your Apple mates. What you might end up losing is messages from your loved ones, which are stored separately on the two systems.

> *Do you like a big screen because you watch movies on your phone? No? Get rid.*

For instance: Do you like a big screen because you watch movies on your phone? No? Get rid. Do you need extra storage because you download programmes and podcasts? No? Let it go! Are pin-sharp photos central to the way you live your life? Don't forget, megapixels relate to the detail in the picture, while lenses indicate the quality of the camera. (For everyday use, 5–8 megapixels per pic is usually deemed sufficient.) If you don't take a lot of sunset selfies, then this is needless expense. Do you really need your phone to be waterproof? If you're starting to say 'hell, no!' to a lot of these questions then don't be tempted to splash out on the top-of-the-range models. You are going to save yourself hundreds of pounds over the course of a two-year contract. Remember, every £5 a month you save is £ 120 back in your pocket. And, repeat after me: that contract <u>will</u> only last two years because…

Handset vs SIM only

Time to unpin that little matter we pinned down earlier. More of us are recognising that upgrading our phones at the earliest opportunity is not just wasteful and eco-spiteful, it's also really, really expensive. The marginal technological gains of our devices just aren't what they were a few years ago, and the cost of paying for a new phone all over again can be eye-watering. That's where the SIM-only contract has made huge headway, encouraging us to keep our two-year-old devices for another 12 months at least, and just pay for calls, texts and data at a fraction of the cost. If you change network you will change SIM (subscriber identity module) card, but keep your number.

Matt Nav

Anecdotal evidence suggests that Apple iPhones have a slightly longer lifespan than their Android counterparts – I've heard estimates of three years vs two. Apple only guarantees its phone working for the duration of the warranty – a year – but for many users it's not a physical breakdown that stops their phone being useful. Software updates introduce new apps and features that older phones can struggle with, reducing operating speeds so the phone isn't practically useful. This goes for both operating systems, but Apple has been the subject of a number of lawsuits from iPhone users who felt they should have got a longer lifespan from their iPhone. All of this is part of the calculation you should make when weighing up a contract, along with the likelihood of going SIM-only at the end.

Pay as you go vs monthly

Once you've chosen the phone you want, it's time to work out the best deal for you. Try to match your contract tariff to how much you'll use the phone. Your current provider (assuming you already have one) will give you an idea of how much data you use, and how many calls and texts you send. If in doubt, shoot slightly high rather than under, as the excess charges are designed to punish rather than gently remind. Also, keep an eye out for things that might be excluded that can also be a bombshell when you get your first bill (damn you, picture messages!). Make sure there's a way to monitor and/or cap your usage and bill so that things don't go doolally without you knowing it. Most providers will send you a text when you're getting close to your limits.

> *Make sure there's a way to monitor and/or cap your usage and bill so that things don't go doolally without you knowing it.*

Now you need to decide whether you want to commit to paying each month, and here's an area where the rapidly changing world of mobile phones is evident. Pay-as-you go contracts used to be a no-brainer for anyone who wanted their mobile on the cheap, without strings attached. You would see teens and the over-sixties rucking with each other to top up their Nokias and Sonys at the post office or newsagents. Not any more, or at least, not as much. Phone companies have made the cost of using these commitment-phobe SIMs much, much higher than before, and started offering other options which have elbowed PAYG into a ditch by the side of the Information Superhighway (™ *Tomorrow's World* c. 1994).

Matt Nav

Phone shop boss Charlie says, 'So many customers just plump for long contracts. I don't get it! If you reckon your phone will last another year, look at the price of a rolling SIM contract and compare that to PAYG or another full year's contract. It will often work out cheaper, and yet you get the freedom to quit at short notice too. If your phone might be nearing the end of its life you'll be able to commit to another longer contract to buy a new one. If your old phone keeps going strong, you're saving money every month. Bonus!'

A second-hand phone or a refurb?

Second-hand phones are tempting. Big names for smaller prices. How protected you are depends on how you buy:

→ Buy from an individual and it's pretty much buyer beware. They don't have to highlight defects because, quite frankly, not being experts, they can't be expected to know about them. Unless they specifically say that a fault doesn't exist, they can't be held responsible.

← Check that it charges, turns on and off and makes noises through the headphones and speaker. Most phones have a series of secret codes that can reveal battery health, memory and other vital stats. Find them out before you see the phone.

→ Buy from a bricks-and-mortar retailer and you're protected by the Consumer Rights Act 2015 (see p. 10). It's got to be SQUAD Fit for Life (see p. 11) – although the lifespan expectation of a second-hand phone is really open to interpretation.

← Buy from an online retailer and you're covered by the CCA (see p. 21). In many ways, this is the safest option as you'll have 14 days to fiddle with the thing and find out what's wrong. Doesn't hurt to remind them of this fact before you buy. Sometimes people... forget.

Refurbs are often sold directly by the manufacturer or retailers, having been properly restored, and they may even arrive in the original box. These phones will come not only with a (possibly shorter) warranty but also with a grading system of A–C, with A being flawless, which will give you a good idea about condition. Accordingly, a refurb phone costs much more than a second-hand one. Whichever you choose, try to chime your purchase with a new phone launch, when there's inevitably an upswell in used models.

3G, 4G or 5G?

Just as the hardware has gone through the gears at an alarming rate, the networks that send and receive our phone signals are racing ahead, trying to make our devices faster and able to handle more data. The G stands for generation and 3G was the third wave of technology that upgraded connectivity in the mobile phone world, launched in 2003. It allowed us to properly access the internet on our phones but it's Billy Basic now, and available on pretty much every phone. Then, in 2012, 4G said, 'Hold on, these guys NEED to watch *Game of Thrones* on the train.' It trounced 3G by being up to five times faster and our commutes were never the same

> *Then, in 2012, 4G said, 'Hold on, these guys NEED to watch Game of Thrones on the train.'*

again. Not all phones can get 4G, and there are parts of the country where you can't get it.

Next on the horizon is 5G, about which the government is making big promises. It's reckoned you could get speeds equivalent to a good internet connection at home, and the time it takes to connect to the network will be reduced. I'm not sure why I would need that, to be honest, but then I'm still getting over text messages. It's only right to say that there is some resistance to this in towns where it's been trialled, because of what's claimed to be a lack of information about the long term health implications of this high-frequency wireless network.

To insure, or not to insure?

When you're sold your phone, there's a good chance someone has tried to flog you insurance to go with it – and it's not cheap. To test whether you need it, ask yourself, 'What type of person am I?' Am I, for instance, the sort of person who regularly drops phones, keys or wallets down drains, toilets or cliffs? If you are, and you still don't fancy the huge monthly expense of insurance, here are a couple of other options:

→ Self-insure. Rather than spend money you'll never get back, stick the equivalent sum into a separate pot in your account. It's there if you, for instance, leave your phone in a pizza box by mistake, and then put it out with the recycling. If you don't need that money for a phone, you can use it for other, more fun things, like buying a sea kayak or having wisdom teeth removed.

← After-market insurance. You probably don't insure your car with the dealership, so why should your phone be any different? Third-party often works out cheaper, and you can choose the cover that works for you. There can be big discounts if you pay for a year up front.

→ Check your home insurance. Many don't cover for accidental loss of phones and other tech, but some do, and yours might be one. You might even be able to add to your policy. A warning: lose your phone overseas and calls made by dodgepots after the event won't be covered, which could be expensive. Also, if you claim this way, there could be an excess to pay, which makes it a waste of time.

← Some 'packaged' bank accounts offer phone (as well as breakdown cover and travel!) insurance as part of their bundle. It's worth weighing up whether the extras are worth the annual fee and hassle of a switch. It might be that the bank you're already with does this, in which case, you could be like Peter Shilton and save in three different directions at the same time.

There's no nice way to put this. In the past, phone insurers have been slippery little critters. On the programme we've heard of lots of cunning ways they use to get out of paying out, and this was inked in by a 2013 Financial Conduct Authority report which found that insurance was being mis-sold and that claims were being paid out reluctantly, if at all. Things have changed a bit for the better as a result, but it's still best to give yourself a fighting chance with your insurer if you need to make a claim. These steps will keep your phone and its contents safer as well, so everyone's a winner, baby:

→ Use a passcode so only you can breach the screen.

← Make a record of the IMEI number, usually found behind the battery, or on the back of Apple products along with the make and model number. You will need this unique set to digits to block the phone if it's lost or stolen.

→ Consider barring calls to international or premium rate numbers on your phone, so you don't incur charges if it is stolen.

← Download an app that can track the whereabouts of your phone. Better still, see if you can get one that will erase content remotely. (This comes as standard on Apple phones.)

→ Register your phone with Immobilise, the UK National Property Register, to help police reunite you with a recovered handset.

← If it's stolen, report the theft immediately – or risk failing in an insurance claim.

→ Back up personal data kept on the phone.

← Only install apps from trusted sources and keep anti-virus protection up to date.

Some policies don't replace lost or stolen phones with new models but refurbs. Indeed, the age of your phone may affect whether it is covered at all. Check the excess on the insurance and be aware that, usually, you will have to send that sum in to the insurance company before any claim is settled. Some insurers ask for the premium to be paid in full before settling. Claims have also been turned down for those without an IMEI number, if the phone has a virus, if the receipt is lost, if cover was taken out more than six months after buying the phone or if 'reasonable care' wasn't shown.

Like I said, slippery little critters.

Roaming

Remember the days when you used to go on holiday with a phone in your pocket and return with a bill running into hundreds of pounds, because you didn't turn off 'mobile data'? An arrangement between EU countries that outlawed roaming charges helped counter that elephant trap but, as Britain leaves the EU, no-one knows what will happen next. Going further afield than the EU, there are already additional costs, as in August 2017 the UK government added a 20 per cent VAT charge to roaming outside the EU on UK-registered devices. The agreement of most phone companies to automatically cap roaming charges at no more than £50 won't change, though. If you are travelling abroad, there are steps you can take to side-step phone costs:

→ When you're abroad use free wifi whenever you can, to reduce communications charges.

← If you are overseas for a while, consider buying a local SIM under a pay-as-you-go arrangement, although you will need an unlocked handset.

→ What about buying a second UK number for your mobile phone, to run alongside your existing one on the same handset? That means you could use it to make calls without risking lengthy incoming calls from distant aunties at premium rates.

← Check what your service provider says about roaming charges so you are informed rather than in debt.

Switching contracts

Breaking up used to be hard to do, sang Neil Sedaka, never. It really did though. Switching your phone provider meant round after round of battles with the retention department as they pleaded with you to stick around, then a painful process of getting your phone unlocked, and squeezing a code out of them. But not any more! Recent changes mean that you don't even need to speak to them. You can just send a little text. For getting rid of life partners, that's harsh. For mobile phone providers, ideal.

So let's do it! Let's STAC and PAC! If you've come to the end of your contract and want out, you need a Service Termination Authorisation Code (STAC) and you can get hold of this by texting STAC to 75075.

And relax. So simple.

Don't think you will have to junk your number, either. All you need is a PAC code (Porting Authorisation Code) from your existing provider to keep the number all your friends from way back have logged. It's their obligation to provide it, and fast. But easier still, just text PAC to 65075 to get your hands on the code. Use it within a month or it will expire.

STAC and PAC, people, STAC and PAC. These changes were introduced in 2019 by Ofcom, to make the playing field that bit more level. Ofcom research found that almost of third of would-be mobile switchers found it difficult to cancel their contracts because of the response of operators. Of those people who decided not to make a change, 45 per cent thought it would be too time consuming and 39 per cent feared it was too much hassle. The ideal time to switch is the very moment your contract expires. Carpe Samsung!

> STAC and PAC, people, STAC and PAC.

However, if you really LOVE talking to retention departments, it's also the A1 moment to haggle with your existing supplier and, if you do have the appetite for a feisty phone call, this is the time to ask for more and better. Yes! It's time once again to become Marvin Haggler! Ding Ding! Round one!

The golden rules of haggling are the same as always:

→ Keep smiling.

← Know what you want, but present it as one of a few options.

→ Don't say yes to the first offer that's made.

← Don't feel the need to fill in the awkward

silences.

See what I did there?

This is where that mega-competitive market works in your favour. Mobile companies will do almost anything to hold on to you. They know that STAC and PAC switching is now quick and easy, and the moment that you walk out the door, looking over your shoulder as you take your business with you, that's the last time you'll have that power for the next two years. Enjoy it, and don't waste it. But don't milk it. It's a phone contract, not a scene from *Downton Abbey*.

It's not quite so straightforward if you are still within the terms of your contract. It's legally binding and getting out is, at the very least, going to cost you money, serious money, if there's still a while to run. If you hate your phone with a vengeance, many providers will offer you early upgrade options to hook you in for another two years. You may be desperate to get out, but chances are that the deal you're getting is pretty wretched. You've signalled to the phone company that you're desperate – never a good look in a negotiation.

Matt Nav

Being the manager of a phone shop is tough. Phones to sell, targets to meet, and all with a smile on your face despite prevailing market conditions. But Charlie does it and he wants you to know how to get the best deal going. So here are his top five tips:

1 Go big or go SIM-only. Buying a phone that's a small upgrade on what you've got makes no sense. You'll still be committing to a two-year contract on a phone that's a marginal improvement and could be redundant by the end. You're better off getting something fresh that will still be current in two years' time, or switching to a low-cost SIM-only deal to save hundreds. Don't mess with Mr In-between.

2 When you buy is crucial. Our big deals come in the January sales, Easter, half-terms, Black Friday or Black Tag – although Black Friday and Black Tag deals now often start the week before, with a guarantee that if the price drops again, you can claim the difference.

3 Deals come and go like judges on *The X Factor*. They're usually because of high stock levels of a certain handset or device. If you see something that looks good, don't hang around for a fortnight, because it will be gone.

4 If a contract is silly cheap, just make sure it's not a refurb – particularly if you're buying online. Some of those guys could make it clearer…

5 Beware the sneaky three-year contract! Some networks are offering that as standard. They can be good value for money, but if your phone doesn't last that long, you're stuck. And a year on a SIM-only can save you hundreds anyway.

Thanks, Charlie! You are a BOSS! Literally.

Selling old mobiles

In 2016, we generated 43 million tonnes of electronic waste globally. That's the weight of 4,500 Eiffel Towers. Some of that cyberclutter may be sitting in a desk drawer in your home, and here's the thing: you could even make a bit of money from it. There are plenty of recycling companies out there who'll make you an offer for your old phone – but whatever you want to turn in, factory reset it to make sure that it's clean of anything that can be used to nick your identity (see identity theft, p. 60). You might find that once they've had a look at your phone they reduce their offer (never raise) and you'll have to make a decision about going ahead. Pull out, and you could pay the delivery costs. Some big retailers offer trade-in deals in-store. They give you a chance to do the whole thing, face to face in real time without getting postie involved.

> *Whatever you want to turn in, factory reset it to make sure that it's clean of anything that can be used to nick your identity.*

Matt Nav

On *Rogue Traders* recently we featured a Manchester-based company who offered to fix phones, laptops, games consoles, tablets and the like for you. At first glance it seemed like a great system, where you could send off the item and, for a fixed fee, they'd diagnose the fault, sort it and send it back within a couple of days. Magic! Why were they on *Rogue Traders* then? Well, in practice, what they did in many cases – including ours – was to receive the item, make up fake problems with it, with a huge bill attached, and then, if you refused to pay that bill, keep your stuff. What a business plan!

In the end, I met one of the main guys in the company as he was on his way back from the gym. It obviously wasn't a legs day as he chose to run away from us for about a mile. Puffed out, he took refuge in a stinky phone box, where he used his mobile to call his minions and shutter the business. Who says landlines don't have their uses?!

BROADBAND

Access to the internet has gone beyond a necessity. It's now defined by the UN as a human right. Too much? Well, it's hard to argue that you're on the same playing field as the rest of society if you don't have it. Nine months in a rental house with no broadband taught me that.

In practice, though, it's subject to the same process as the rest of our utilities: sold to us by private companies who compete to offer us better or worse services for more or less money. As our access to employment, healthcare, banking, education, government, news, entertainment and the outside world in general becomes more dependent on the internet, it's important that you get a deal that keeps you patched in and up to speed at the best price possible.

Broadly speaking (ahem), there are three types of broadband. ADSL stands for Asymmetric Digital Subscriber Line. It flows through copper wires, and that means the speed you get is largely dependent on how far you live from the local telephone exchange. Effectively, your internet is being delivered by donkey and cart, via the scenic route.

Then there are cable networks, dominated by Virgin in the UK. These use hair-thin and lightning-fast fibre optics for most of the journey, then coaxial cable for the last bit from the box in the street to your home. It's a lot quicker than copper wires. Your donkey has been replaced by the favourite in the 2.30 at Kempton Park.

Finally there's superfast fibre optic broadband. That's what you get up to the box in the street. After that it's either copper wire or, in a few cases, fibre optic cable straight into your house. So, it's either Billy Whizz right up to that box, and then a sedate donkey ride for the last few yards, or blink-and-you-missed-it speed straight into your router.

Sadly, whatever the sales pitch says, the chances are you won't have much choice. Coverage for all types of broadband is not nationwide and there's no guarantee it's going to be in your neighbourhood any time soon. Ofcom have a broadband coverage checker so you can discover what's promised in your postcode – definitely worth doing before you shop for a new deal, as it's changing all the time.

But if you're sitting trying to watch a stuttering episode of *Mrs Brown's Boys* on iPlayer, don't despair. A few tweaks around your house and you might be able to boost broadband speeds yourself. They might not make it Usain Bolt, but you might get Mo Farah. Running downhill.

➔ Update your browser as an old version could be putting the brakes on your broadband.

> *They might not make it Usain Bolt, but you might get Mo Farah.*

← Check there are no recently installed electrics causing interference. Routers need to be isolated as far as possible from any other electrics, especially the wireless kind. Even telephone extension leads can have an effect, as can coiled or tangled cables. Lightning may also cause issues but these, of course, will resolve themselves.

→ If your router is ageing, ask for a new one from your provider. This works particularly well when you come to renew your contract (see Marvin Haggler, above).

← Be sure your security is up to date so that a cheeky neighbour can't tune in and nick half your bandwidth. Change passwords, and if necessary, change your router name to 'Oi, Kevin! Get your own wifi!'

→ Go old school and use a LAN ethernet cable to connect computer to router, rather than using wifi. If you want, you can use PowerLine adapters to run the internet through your power sockets for the rest of the house.

← Crackly phone lines will take a toll on broadband speeds so make sure you have modern sockets and microfilters – white boxes that split phone and broadband signals – where necessary.

→ There are gizmos available designed to help by filtering out interference, so look into using a broadband accelerator.

← Turn your router off and on again. Sometimes this will kick-start everything, but don't resort to this too often and certainly don't do it on a daily basis.

→ Move yourself and your computer closer to the router.

← Clear your browser's cache as the data drags speeds down.

→ Remember, a security download will grind on a computer's gears, so make allowances for that. Also, there's often congestion at peak times.

← If you don't get the promised service you should be able to cancel without penalty.

Matt Nav

Internet service providers are like kids in a pedal car, imagining they're travelling at speeds that they know they can't deliver. We used to regularly feature stories about unrealistic advertised speeds which then didn't add up for customers once they'd signed on the dotted line. This was, in part at least, because up until May 2018 ISPs were allowed to advertise speeds of 'up to' a certain figure (measured in megabits per second or Mbps). To justify those speeds, they had to show that just 10 per cent of users were able to get them, a bit like advertising that everybody can be as attractive as Daniel Craig because Daniel Craig is, demonstrably, a 9 out of 10.

Nonsense, nonsense, nonsense. Anyway, since that day in May 2018, ISPs can only advertise average speeds – a median speed taken at peak usage times. Typically, this would bring down a speed of 18 Mbps to something more like 11. You've gone from Daniel Craig to Steve Buscemi. OK, your broadband is still kinda hot, in its own unique way, but our expectations have been managed down.

Don't take your provider's word for the speeds you're getting. Checking is easy. Ofgem have a simple measure that takes about 30 seconds to complete (if the broadband is functioning well) and there are plenty of others available online. It's probably a good idea to do the test more than once, at different times of day, to get a decent across-the-board figure. If your broadband is underperforming, don't hesitate to make contact with your provider. Most providers have signed up to a code of practice that provides a minimum speed guarantee. If you think the problem is their end and it's not fixed in 30 days, you can exit your contract without paying a price.

And guess what? There's an agreed scheme of automatic compensation among some providers that means you will get money back when the system goes wrong, to the tune of £8 for every calendar day that the service isn't serving. The cash should show on your bill within a month. Again, Ofgem have all the details.

What's that you say? You'd like to include a landline in that package? Why, don't mind if I do!

LANDLINES

Landlines are hanging on, just. Around half as many of us are using landline calls now as we were back in 2012, says Ofcom. It's hardly surprising. Advances in the mobile network mean we can get everything we need and more from our portable devices – including free calls over the internet. It makes pay-per-minute calls over a scratchy connection look – and sound – distinctly 1987.

It's still reassuring to have a landline though. Pinning everything on your mobile signal or internet provider means you're at their mercy, and in those rural areas where providers haven't quite got their act together, a landline is often a lifeline.

Beware though, landline charges can be a sting in the tail. It's fair to say that landlines are a bit of an afterthought now for a lot of providers, but like other utilities such as gas or electricity, providers will balance the fixed monthly

> *Pinning everything on your mobile signal or internet provider means you're at their mercy.*

charge you pay for your package against usage. If you're on a Billy Basic broadband bundle, you can pretty much guarantee they'll be trying to make some money back on extended calls to your mum before teatime. It may feel like a cheap evening call, but make that call in peak time (for example, before 7pm for BT) and it could be mucho moolah. A single, long call every month can make it worth considering paying monthly to cover the lot.

NUISANCE CALLS AND MESSAGES

Why on earth do they think we'll fall for it? A call from a Warrington number (for some reason it's always Warrington) with a recorded introduction which says they know all about the accident we've just had. But when, curious to find out more, we get connected, the next person clearly knows nothing about this accident, and tries to pull off a stage spiritualist trick to get us to share more details.

Whether it's accident insurance claims, loft insulation or 'market research', these calls only happen because they work – particularly for the most vulnerable in our society. To prevent a nuisance for you, or a menace to someone you love, here are a few simple steps:

→ Cold calling isn't illegal. Continuing to call once you've been told to stop is. Try to identify the caller by dialling 1471 or looking at the caller display, make a note of how many times you are being called and complain to Ofcom.

← Consider using an anonymous call rejection service, so that unidentified callers are rejected. There are several blocking services commercially available.

→ Join the telephone preference service, which should end cold calls from reputable sources made from Britain. Everything else is either outside the UK, dodgepots, or, most likely, a bit of both. Remember, OOTBNFY!

← Install an answerphone and let it do the heavy lifting.

For spam text messages:

→ If the message comes from a short code (just 5 figures) then text back STOP. This should mean you don't get any more.

← Longer than 5 figures? Don't get back in touch. That tells them there's someone at the end of the line.

→ Report the number by forwarding it to Ofcom on 7726.

Matt Nav

Ofcom don't muck about. They take cold calling seriously and issue massive fines when they catch firms at it. The biggest was in 2018. A company called Miss-sold Products Ltd (the clue is in the title!) was fined £100,000 for automated cold calling. Impressive, right? Well, yes, until you learn that they made 75 million unsolicited calls. So that's a fine of just over 0.001p per call. Still! Good work, Ofcom! Keep it up!

TV

More and more, what TV you get is determined by who your ISP might be. The bundles of entertainment packages all need a good broadband signal to get them onto the screen, so don't bother with them if your internet is delivered by donkey, sloth or snail. Sub 2 Mbps and as far as TV is concerned, you are inter<u>not</u>.

It's also worth asking yourself if you need 300 channels. Another approach is to have one of the free-to-air services (Freesat if you've got a dish, or Freeview for an antenna) and add streaming services on top. You'll need a PVR box to catch 'em, but it should also give you access to BBC iPlayer and other catch-up services. Quite frankly, there's only so much time in the day to watch telly, and this way you can dip in and out of the things you love, without watching that inflated monthly bill drop on the mat for programmes you've never seen. Honestly? It's what I do.

Matt Nav

Yes, it's called a TV licence, but it isn't just for TVs. If you watch or record any programmes as they are being shown, on any channel, and on any device, you will need to get one. If you watch on BBC iPlayer, you'll need one too. Blind people and those in residential care don't have to pay. Free TV licences for the over 75s funded by the government are coming to an end in August 2020 (perhaps), although the BBC will help those on pension credit. This could change at some point in the future, but quite frankly, I've probably said too much already.

chapter
six

Renting and Buying a Home

There's nothing better you can do with your time and money than find somewhere decent for you and your family to live. It's a platform for living, loving and learning. After all, what's the point in having a flash car and smart clothes if you have nowhere to park and your closets are damp? Employment, relationships, education, health – all of these will suffer if you don't have a home that looks after you, your loved ones and your stuff. So let's get a roof over your head!

It won't be easy though. The housing market right now is loopy. Sometimes it can seem that the odds are stacked against you ever renting or buying somewhere you'll love, and there are dodgepot landlords and letting agents who can use your desperation against you. Once again, those who are in the greatest need are often those who end up getting swindled. Let's have a look at your options, and what to do if you've run out of options.

At their peak in the late 1970s there were over 5 million council properties available. Now there are just over a million.

COUNCIL HOUSING

Remember that? Once councils provided homes for people who couldn't afford to buy and they were plentiful too – uninterrupted streets of them and blocks of flats high into the sky. At their peak in the late 1970s there were over 5 million council properties available. Now there are just over a million. There's an acute shortage, with the homeless charity Shelter estimating that 1.2 million people are on the waiting list for social housing.

But hold on! The tower blocks and streets are mostly still there, so what's the problem? Well, in the early '80s the government introduced the Right To Buy your own council property, which people did enthusiastically, turning council properties into private homes. Great news for council tenants, who became homeowners, not so great for councils, who still had, and have, a legal obligation to house the people on their patch.

There are lots of good reasons to want a council house. Local authorities are social landlords, which means tenancies should be long term and secure. The rent (social rent) is also usually much cheaper than the private sector, and because they're the landlord, the council comes out to repair problems when they occur, at no cost to you.

It's difficult – but not impossible – to get a council house. The first step is to make an application to your local council, either online or on paper. To be considered you first have to meet immigration criteria and comply with the council's own regulations. Remember, one council's approach may vary from the next here, even if they are neighbours. Should your application be successful you will end up on a waiting list, but even then there's no guarantee of a property turning up. If your circumstances are critical, you may get onto a priority list, which will surely improve your chances of success. You don't have to accept the first offer of a home, but repeated refusals are likely to see you bumped down the list, or even off of it – although you can appeal.

Council home tenancies usually begin with a 12-month trial period, which is followed either by long-term secure tenancies or sometimes fixed-period, flexible arrangements. After that first year you will be able to rent out rooms, swap homes with another council house tenant and, after three years, even purchase that property through the Right to Buy scheme. You might also be able to carry out modifications, after checking with the council. The Spare Room Subsidy, introduced in 2013 (sometimes called the Bedroom Tax) means that your benefits will be reduced if you have a bedroom you're not using.

HOMELESSNESS

If you are homeless or about to be evicted, your local council has to step in to help, in theory, anyway. Housing officers should work with you to find accommodation for at least eight weeks after you make what's called a 'homeless application'. It's always best to go in person to visit the housing department and take with you proof of identity, any relevant tenancy agreement, eviction notice or medical information. You can ask for help even if you have got a roof over your head if your circumstances are a bit grim, for example, if you're sofa surfing or your accommodation is overcrowded. These are tricky encounters. It's best to get advice before you go in, however desperate things are (see the section on intentional homelessness, p. 189).

What will you end up with? Well, you may qualify for emergency housing, which could be a bed and breakfast, a hostel or a self-contained flat. Councils should try to keep people in their local area so they remain close to work, family or healthcare, but sometimes

> Councils should try to keep people in their local area so they remain close to work, family or healthcare, but sometimes that's not possible.

Matt Nav

How can you be **intentionally homeless**? Believe me, it's a thing. Councils do have a duty to house the people they serve, and each will have a policy for allocating housing, which should be publicly available. Typically, you stand a better chance if you are homeless, living in poor or overcrowded conditions or trying to get away from danger – for instance, domestic abuse. Watch out though: councils often don't have capacity for even these top priorities. Some councils will be over-eager to categorise you as 'intentionally homeless', meaning that something you did – or didn't do – led to you losing your home. This could include leaving before you're evicted, or failing to pay your rent. In those circumstances your chances of getting help to be housed drop dramatically, and you're on your own. Brutal, but that's the way housing can be right now. Before you present yourself to the council, get advice from Citizens Advice or Shelter. They'll make sure you give yourself the best chance of getting the council to do their bit.

that's not possible. I've met people who've been relocated 50 miles away because of a housing shortage close to home. Once you've been away from their area for a while, you are no longer the responsibility of the council that put you there. For cash-strapped councils, it's a great way to pass the buck, but it can have the effect of permanently separating families from their support and leaving them at risk. If you are offered something outside your neighbourhood you can challenge the housing department decision.

HOUSING ASSOCIATIONS

Taking up a huge chunk of the slack left by the demise of the council flat are housing associations. These are usually non-profit organisations, sometimes charities, whose purpose is to provide people with affordable homes. Back at the peak of the council flat in the late '70s, there were under half a million HA properties. Now there are around 2.5 million.

Matt Stat

In 1979 social housing (council and housing association) provided 32 per cent of UK housing stock. Now it's around half that.

Housing associations, like the council, are social landlords, providing low-cost rented homes. Very often they'll work closely with local authorities to make sure that they're doing the most good, getting roofs over the heads of people in greatest need. However, it's really worth approaching housing associations separately from your council application. Many take applications directly, and may have their own criteria and ideas (shared ownership, staged ownership) which you wouldn't necessarily find out about from the council.

A version of Right To Buy – Right To Acquire (wow, such a difference!) – now applies to housing association properties, meaning tenants can buy their properties at a discount once they've been living there for long enough. If you think that home ownership is very important, you'll applaud this. If you think maintaining a stock of property at affordable social rents is important, you won't. From 2020, social landlords, like councils and housing associations, in England will be able to increase rents annually, by no more than the rate of inflation plus 1 per cent. If it's a new build, they're allowed to charge up to 80 per cent of a market rent.

PRIVATE RENTALS

As the stocks of social housing have diminished and the cost of owning your own home has spiralled out of reach for many, private landlords are now providing a roof over the heads of millions of people they never used to. There are now 4.5 million privately rented households, each of which could comprise any number of individuals. It's not just your starter outers either: the proportion of 35–54-year-olds who live as private tenants has nearly doubled in a decade, according to government figures, often as a result of unexpected personal crises like death, debt or divorce.

> Housing charity Shelter claims that almost half of England's 8.5 million private renters experience stress or anxiety thanks to unaffordable rents, poor living conditions and the overarching threat of eviction.

There are, of course, many private landlords who offer accommodation of an excellent standard to contented tenants. But I tend to hear about the bad apples you need to guard against. Housing charity Shelter claims that almost half of England's 8.5 million private renters experience stress or anxiety thanks to unaffordable rents, poor living conditions and the overarching threat of eviction.

Most people who rent will have Assured Shorthold Tenancies (AST) which can give you relative security for six months, and the right for tenants to call their front door their own. The landlord can issue a 'no-fault' Section 21 notice to seek repossession of the property at the end of that (you have a couple of months' notice to quit) and, after a brief court hearing (at which you can make a representation), you have to go. If you've broken the terms of your tenancy, they can stick in an 'it IS your fault' Section 8 notice as well, saying that there are grounds to get you out. Failing to pay your rent and anti-social behaviour are a couple of these reasons. Sections 21 and 8 of the Housing Act give landlords a lot of power. They shouldn't be trying to get you out any other way, through coercion or threats. These notices have to go through the courts too. If they haven't bothered then these notices aren't worth anything. Your best bet to make sure your landlord is not trying to speed you out the door is to speak to Shelter. They are masters at adding a bit of friction to your eviction.

Matt Nav

Landlords often make mistakes on Section 21 notices. Not giving enough notice, failure to protect your deposit, a failure to licence a building that needs one (see houses in multiple occupation, p. 201) or a failure to go to court in time will all render the notice invalid. These rules are there to protect you, so make sure your landlord sticks to them. Not everyone has an AST though. If your tenancy is pre-MC Hammer (1989) then hey, Section 21! You can't touch this! However, if you live in the same property as your landlord, then you're not a tenant, with all the associated rights – you're a lodger, Roger. They can get you out lickety-split with a week or two's notice, and there's no need to go to court at all, because at the end of the day, it's their gaff, their rules.

Escalating rents are proving a problem. Most tenancy agreements feature a rent review clause, or a landlord may issue a Section 13 notice, warning of an increase. It is possible to challenge rent levels through a tribunal. Find details about it on the Section 13 paperwork and don't hang around, as your application has to be submitted before the rent increase takes effect. Also, consult Citizens Advice to explore your options. A Section 21 notice is sometimes a preface to a rent rise. You're instantly in a weaker negotiating position on rent if you know you might soon have to move and scrape together a new deposit. These notices have also proved an effective way of shutting up tenants who justifiably complain about problems with the property – so-called 'revenge evictions'. The government has promised to curb their powers in England, saying landlords will only be able to use Section 21 notices when there's a good reason to get rid of a tenant. Wales is set to follow suit while in Scotland landlords have been barred from acting on a whim since 2017. It seems to me though that the threat of eviction is a bit like carrying a chainsaw round in a shopping centre. You don't have to use it to get people out of the way.

> *These notices have also proved an effective way of shutting up tenants who justifiably complain.*

Section 21 to one side, some private landlords make an art form of providing rotten living conditions, but many people still don't realise that if the roof is leaking or there's mould growing on the walls, you don't have to be a council tenant to involve the local authority. All landlords are legally bound to comply with the Housing Health and Safety Rating System, introduced by the Housing Act of 2004, a risk assessment form which should highlight any serious dangers. Councils enforce this and a recent overhaul of HHSRS is leading to changes that will make it easier for local authorities to act than ever before. Let's hope it puts the rogues out of vogue.

Letting agents

Gotta love a middle man or woman. Getting in the middle there and making life more complicated and expensive. OK, there are probably really good reasons for letting agents, but their legacy over the last few years has been a string of eye-watering fairy-tale charges and fees that seem to spring out of nowhere. Viewing fees, costs for setting up a tenancy, or ending one, one charge for professional cleaning at the end of a tenancy and another if the moving day was Saturday – just a few I've heard of. Those days are (almost) gone, thanks to the Tenants' Fees Act of 2019. Now, all a tenant can be charged is the rent and a refundable deposit, paid back at the end of the tenancy minus any agreed costs.

Matt Nav

I got into programmes about housing because of a letting agent in North West London who came up with a cunning plan: show numerous desperate renters the same flat, and take deposits and fees from all of them, but – and here's the really clever bit – never rent out the flat. When it comes to moving day, just disappear to rent out another place to hoodwink the homeless and scrape your fees off the top. Meanwhile your renters all turn up on the doorstep, with boxes packed in a van, and nowhere to sleep that night, thousands of pounds down. We secretly filmed this process, and then confronted him during a viewing. He threatened to jump off the balcony and said it would be our fault. I was fairly confident he had no plan to do this as he would have landed directly on the roof of his late-plate Mercedes S-Class parked downstairs. As with all big-money transactions, SDCD: a snap decision is a cr*p decision. Don't put yourself in a situation where you have to hand over money to someone who has nothing to lose by simply driving away in their lovely motor.

Before you sign any agreement or hand over money, you need to know how much the rent is and when it is due, who to contact about repairs and, indeed, whether you must pay a tenancy deposit. This is usual but the money you hand over is just that: a deposit. Dodgepot landlords have traditionally seen this as a lovely present, knowing they can find a host of petty damages which miraculously add up to exactly that sum when you move out. Not any more! Legally, at least. The cash now has to be deposited in one of a handful of government-backed tenancy deposit schemes within 30 days, and you, as tenant must be told which one. At payback time, it should be back with you ten days after any sum for damages has been agreed. If there's a dispute, the deposit stays safe in the scheme until that's resolved, with the good people at the deposit scheme ready to act as adjudicators. If your landlord failed to use the deposit scheme as required, then you should be in line for compensation of between one and three times the total.

> *The cash now has to be deposited in one of a handful of government-backed tenancy deposit schemes within 30 days.*

Here's the stress-free five-step guide to renting:

➡ View the property in person and meet the landlord.

⬅ Ensure the landlord uses a government-approved deposit protection scheme.

➡ Insist on an inventory and a report about the condition of the place, preferably with photos.

⬅ Make sure the inventory is signed by both sides.

➡ If anything looks like a fee, tell them to sling their hook.

Houses in Multiple Occupation (HMOs)

For HMOs, read bedsits. These are bedrooms in a house where you share cooking and bathing facilities with other people who you may not know. Students, young professionals and the recently divorced often find themselves living at close quarters, but importantly, HMOs come in two sizes. Anywhere with at least three tenants from different families sharing facilities is just an HMO, while if there are five tenants it's classed as a large HMO and needs a licence from the council, and there are stricter regulations. HMOs meet a need, but because they're housing individuals living separately, they need to be managed really carefully. In the case of a fire, for instance, it's less likely that you'll each know who's in and who's out, so alarm systems have to work in every area, and be mains powered to avoid the batteries running out without being replaced. Again, Shelter and the council will tell you what to expect. If your place is not up to scratch, then don't ignore it – it's not just your life at risk.

Spot a bad pad

If you rent a property then your landlord must keep you safe. Here's the tick list of their responsibilities:

➡ Give you a copy of the gas safety check record as you move in or within 28 days of the check taking place. This shows the gas and everything it flows through are all working safely (if there is gas).

⬅ Make sure the electrics work safely. HMOs need an inspection every five years.

➡ Make sure there are smoke alarms on each level as a minimum. Large HMOs need more than this.

⬅ Make sure there are protected escape routes.

➡ Any furniture provided must be fire-resistant.

⬅ HMOs must have enough cooking and bathroom facilities for all occupants.

➡ Communal areas have to be clean, smart and lit.

⬅ Bins and rubbish bags must be provided.

BUYING
A HOME

*Right. Straight to the other end of the spectrum.
Somehow you've navigated your way through renting
and drummed up a deposit.*

Bleeding obvious fact, houses are well expensive,
but here's the thing no-one tells you: the cost of the
mortgage is just the Christmas tree. Hanging off it on
every branch of this process are shiny expensive money
baubles and strings of cash tinsel you'll need to spend
that also need to be part of your calculations. House-
buying technicalities differ in Scotland, Wales, Northern
Ireland and England. This piece focuses on England but
should give you an idea of where extra costs will be
incurred, wherever you live. Equally, it's impossible to say
how expensive each step will be as that depends on the
size of property you are buying and whereabouts it is in
the country. So if you see this sign – £££ – expect to dip
into your bank account, again.

Mortgages

Eventually, most of us will want to live in a home of our own. Unless we are heirs to a fortune, that means taking out a home loan or mortgage. The first time feels pretty daunting, tying yourself into decades of debt for sums you can't imagine ever earning, but the beauty of the mortgage is that while you live in your home, you're investing all the time in the thing that you'll use the most. Also, historically, property has gained value, and the chances are at the end of your mortgage term you will look back at the sum you committed to 25 years earlier and think it was a bargain, certainly when compared to paying rent to a private landlord.

There are a few main types of mortgage with endless variations and combinations:

→ **Fixed.** You'll pay a set Annual Percentage Rate (APR) every year, broken down into monthly payments. This fixed element is typically for the first two, three or five years, after which you flick back to...

← **Variable.** Your APR is the Standard Variable Rate (SVR) of your lender. This is, typically, not a great thing, as it will sit somewhere above the fixed deal you worked out. Lenders can change this whenever they want, not just when the Bank of England puts up its base rate. Probably time to switch for a new deal.

➜ **Tracker.** This is linked to the Bank of England's base rate, which they review on the first Thursday of every month. When I say linked, I mean that your APR will track up and down with it, but usually at some percentage points' distance. As an example, if the Bank of England base rate is 1 per cent, and your deal tracks at +2 per cent of that base rate, you'll pay 3 per cent. If the Bank of England sticks it at 3 per cent, you'll pay 5 per cent. This is great if, as we've seen over the past few years, Bank of England base rate has been set at fractions of a percent. If and when it rises, expect to see everyone scrabble for the safe high ground of a fixed-rate mortgage.

REPAYMENT OR INTEREST ONLY?

With each and any of these mortgages, you'll also be given two options: you can pay off the whole sum borrowed, by chipping away at the debt each month (a repayment or capital & interest mortgage), leaving you with a home you own at the end of the process, or you can just pay the interest (interest only), meaning that you'll either need to find a way to pay off the loan at the end of the term, or start collecting cardboard boxes, because you're outta there. For many people, 25 or 30 years can seem like a long way away. It soon creeps up on you, and as I often tell my son, if you don't have a plan, you soon become part of someone else's.

> *If you don't have a plan, you soon become part of someone else's.*

The mortgage deal you'll get is dependent on a few things, but one of the most crucial is the Loan to Valuation ratio (LTV). Your lender will look at the value of the house, and the sum they're loaning, and want to know the ratio between the two. Take out a £150,000 mortgage to buy a £300,000 home and your LTV is 50 per cent. You're a pretty safe bet, because their investment is pretty secure, whatever happens to you, and to house prices. With this ratio you're likely to get pretty good APRs and, possibly, lower fees. If you're buying the same home with just £15,000 down, you will not get the same deals and will pay higher APRs. Don't worry! As you keep paying off that mortgage (and on the assumption that over time, prices go up) before you know it your LTV ratio will have sorted itself out and you'll have value built up in your home, which I like to call equity. In fact, it's not just me. Everyone calls it equity.

BROKER OR BANKER?

When it comes to getting mortgage advice there are a couple of paths. It's best to get a general idea of what's about by looking at a comparison website first. Then, if you reckon you've spotted the best deal, you can march

Matt Nav

The incredible pressure in recent years to get on the housing ladder has opened the door to some really gruesome scams. A couple of series ago we featured a building company that was targeting people who desperately wanted to buy, but didn't have the necessaries to drum up the deposit. The housebuilders lent them the deposit, but convinced them to lie on the mortgage application, saying that the deposit had come as a gift from a family member. Not only were the builders pulling a fast one, they were convincing people that lying on the form was perfectly standard, and, crucially, was the only way to secure their own home. The houses themselves were shoddily built, and overpriced to make sure the builder didn't lose out on the deposit scam. But the homeowners were stuck, knowing that if they complained or went public, they could be accused of mortgage fraud. Nasty, nasty business.

straight into the lender's branch, find an advisor and declare your undying love for their product.

Instead, I'd suggest visiting them and letting them know that theirs is among a few products you are considering. You like some aspects, but not others. You are into Marvin Haggler territory here, although there might not be too much to fight for. Lenders have been known to negotiate on their headline rates, but it's as rare a sighting as Theresa May at samba lessons. Where you might find a little wiggle room is on the fees charged. These are an important part of the mortgage melange, and can run into the thousands. Always ask if those are in any way negotiable. And even if you're sure it's the right mortgage, walk away... because SDCD.

I'll be honest, this is not my favourite approach. By law, mortgage advisors for banks and building societies can only talk about their own products, and it's a big old financial world out there. If you can, develop a friendship with an independent mortgage advisor, who can give you the flavour of the whole market, and will even give you a call if they see a deal that looks good for you. I did this with my first mortgage, and a shared love of punk and new-wave music has meant that he is now one of my best friends. Why this is good for you is because it means he has deigned to share his incredible wisdom with you now. Ladies and gentlemen: the world's greatest mortgage advisor/punk band frontman, Rockin' Bob.

Matt Nav

Rockin' Bob says:

- Lenders don't care what you've paid as rent for the last five years. They have to make their own assessment of what you can afford. If you've been handing over £1,500 a month, that doesn't mean they'll give you a £1,500-a-month mortgage.

- Don't pay for a survey straight away. They're well expensive! Let the lender carry out their valuation first – it's usually free. Get the offer before you spend more on people prodding walls.

- Parents can help out, but rarely as guarantors. The old system where a parent's signature used to help secure your loan if you're not making enough moolah doesn't work any more. Now lenders will want to see the colour of their money, either as a gift from their savings, or by committing their savings to your purchase for a few years. Alternatively, and gaining popularity these days, is releasing some of the equity in their own property to gift to you, to use as a deposit against yours.

You see? I told you he was good! Apart from knowing all the chords for 'London Calling', independent mortgage advisors have another great advantage: over the years they have built up relationships of trust with the lenders with whom they deal. They get paid commission for every mortgage they broker, and it's important for them to get the business away. They have been known to be Marvin Haggler on your behalf to get the very best deal possible, sometimes even reducing fees. More than this, find a good advisor and they just make the whole process less painful, telling you what needs to be done and when. Sometimes it's good to have a gentle reminder.

Right. Let's get this thing done! Start by running a credit check (see p. 143) to make sure there's nothing that's going to hold you back here. Find out if you're eligible for one of the range of affordable home-buying schemes. If you're a first-time buyer there are some really useful schemes which can open doors which might have remained closed.

HELP TO BUY

How about this? Buy a new-build home for under £600,000. You raise 5 per cent of the value of your new home as a deposit. Under the Help To Buy scheme, the government then loans you another 20 per cent at a cracking low rate of interest – interest free for the first five years, in fact – which you can repay at any time.

You now have a virtual 25 per cent deposit, meaning you get access to lower mortgage rates. OK, it's worth pointing out that there is a downside. Five years can go by pretty quickly, at the end of which that interest kicks in. It might not be much, but it builds over time, and if your budget is tight, it might be the straw that breaks the camel's back. Don't kick the debt down the road unless you've worked out how you're going to get yourself out of it. Help To Buy comes to an end in March 2021, but it will be replaced by something a bit similar until 2023.

> *Don't kick the debt down the road unless you've worked out how you're going to get yourself out of it.*

Finding the right house or flat

To get some idea of affordability, use one of the many mortgage calculators available online. It's also worth working out what would happen if your circumstances change, for instance, if you or your partner was out of work for a while (I'll warn you now, children do happen) or if there's a change in interest rates. Set yourself some hard boundaries on affordability before you start looking at properties. It's really easy to get swept up by a property and land yourself in a heap of debt.

Now for the fun bit: scrolling through page after page on the internet and virtually walking through the rooms, weighing up location, schools, transport links, storage, parking, orientation, outside space and, most important of all, the colour of the bathroom. The old adage is true. Top of your list should always be location, location, location. An area might be up and coming, but if it's been up and coming for 30 years, the chances of it happening in your time are slim. A great tool is the HM Land Registry's price paid data search: https://www.gov.uk/search-house-prices. That gives you an idea of the price history of the property you're looking at, along with other similar ones in the street. It's a fantastic negotiating tool, and if prices

> The old adage is true. Top of your list should always be location, location, location.

Matt Nav

If you take nothing else from this chapter, please, PLEASE be aware of **conveyancing fraud**, which is on the up and can come from all directions. Fraudsters can impersonate buyers, sellers, lenders and solicitors, with the aim of getting in between the different parties and intercepting the huge sums of money that are being transferred in any property transaction (see the section on authorised push payment fraud, p. 40). Faked emails, websites, letterheads, phone numbers – all of these are open to scam artists, so make sure you start with contact details you trust, and if they change, for ANY reason, go back through those trusted channels to check you're dealing with who you think you are. Imagine you're physically handing over £15,000 to someone. You'd want to look them right in the eye, and know their shoe size, right? However rushed and stressed you may feel, take that Brad Pitt, ultra-cool moment and make sure you know who you're really sending your life savings to.

have flatlined you'll want to know why. Then go to www. police.co.uk and scare yourself rigid by looking at the crime figures for your prospective street. It's worth taking these with a pinch of salt, because a report of anti-social behaviour can mean a row that comes to nothing and gets sorted before police arrive. Don't freak yourself out.

Finally, check your council's planning register. If there's an incinerator planned for your back garden, you'll want to know about it as early as possible, certainly before you've spent hundreds on a solicitor to tell you something you could have found out yourself with a couple clicks. As *The X-Files* said, the truth is out there!

So yes, you'll need a solicitor to sort out the legalities of the purchase (£££). Although you won't have to pay the whole cost initially, most will ask for a deposit. It's also the solicitor's job to conduct searches on the neighbourhood you want to buy in, to check if there's a pig farm proposed next door and no motorway planned at the bottom of the garden (£££).

Surveys

There are a couple of different types here. Because they're no mugs, your lender will sensibly want to survey the property to ensure it's worth the money they're giving you (£££). This report is for them, not you. If the lender thinks the place is over-priced, they may not give you all the money you need to buy it. Then you have two options: either bin the whole sale, or, if you're brave, use this info to go back to the negotiating table. Lender's surveys tend to be fairly cursory though, so if they say it's a dud, it's probably got a wall hanging off. If you're still serious about the property, you'll probably be interested in your own survey on top of this.

I feel terribly conflicted about surveys because, in my experience, they tend to be quite limited in what they achieve. There are two levels of survey above the lender's basic report: a homebuyer's report (££££££) or a structural survey (£££££££££). Even the most expensive surveys don't necessarily include a valuation of the property, although you can ask for one. My real problem with surveys is how much wiggle room they sometimes leave the surveyor. Every survey I've seen has a list of excluded activities, for instance, lifting carpets or inspecting the loft space, which means that hidden defects like rotten floors or holey roofs stay hidden. Here's a test: when booking your surveyor, ask if it's OK for you to join them while they carry out their inspection. The best ones will let you, as long as you don't ask too many daft questions and are

> *Here's a test: when booking your surveyor, ask if it's OK for you to join them while they carry out their inspection.*

prepared to hold their ladder (they should have a ladder, a torch and a damp meter). In my experience, many won't agree to it. I don't get this. You're paying, and it's a really important process. The survey, if it's carried out correctly, does a couple of things: it points out if this property deserves a swerve, or gives you points for negotiation further down the line. In short, it's like the corkscrew in your kitchen drawer: of limited use, but you wouldn't want to be without it.

The chain (not Fleetwood Mac)

This is when the house-buying process can drive you to distraction. You see, above and below your transaction (unless you're a first-time buyer) there is probably a string of other transactions taking place, as your seller moves into another property, and, if you're selling, the person below you moves out of theirs. These chains can stretch across dozens of transactions, until someone moves into an empty property (vacant possession) at the top end, or is a first-time-buyer at the bottom. The whole thing can fall apart with a single failed negotiation or rejected mortgage, resulting in thousands wasted on surveys and solicitors. This is when effective communication with your estate agent is crucial. Sometimes the chain falls apart. It's heartbreaking, but you just have to accept it, pick yourself up and start again.

Estate agents

The good, and unexpected, news here is that there are some great estate agents. There are also a few stinkers. For either, it's important to understand how they work: on commission, and on behalf of the seller. But 1.5 per cent commission on nothing is nothing, so on the whole, it's more important for them to make the sale and meet their targets than it is to boost the price by another £500. To make yourself as attractive as possible to the agent, make it clear that you have your ducks lined up in a row and ready to go, and that, in classic Marvin Haggler style, you have other properties you're looking at. Then ask them as many questions as you can think of about the property. There are no bad or stupid questions while your deposit is still in your pocket. Remember, the estate agent may be your ally, but they are not your friend.

Can't think of any questions? Well, don't worry, because if you're buying a flat Rockin' Bob has already thought of a few:

→ Is it leasehold or freehold? How many years are on the lease? Fewer than 70 and you might struggle to get a mortgage.

← Who is the freeholder (property and land)? Owning a share of the freehold can be good, as the number of years left on the lease is less important, but it does mean you'll have to co-operate with other owners to get big stuff (roofs, drains) fixed.

→ Is there a management company to look after all the shared bits? If so, what's the annual service charge? If you're buying a flat, the service charge can be a huge monthly chunk, not the sort of thing you want to find out when you've already committed.

← What are the neighbours like? Is the block privately owned, or a mix of private and council tenants? This is not by any means a judgement on council tenants, but sometimes lenders can refuse a mortgage if very little of the block is in private ownership.

→ How long has the property been on the market? If it's more than a couple of months, the estate agent had better have a good reason.

Extra costs

So, the estate agent has answered all your questions, you are happy with the property and BINGO! You've received your mortgage offer. This is where you'll really start to notice those expensive baubles on the tree. You'll usually pay the lender an arrangement fee (£££). Then it will be time to exchange contracts via solicitors, who usually ask for a deposit to back up the pledge to buy (£££). After exchange (at exchange is better), you'll need building insurance to cover the structure of the property (£££).

As the purchase completes, the money being used as a deposit is wired to the seller's solicitor (£££). A mortgage account fee may well kick in (£££) alongside the solicitor's final bill (£££), and there will be a further amount to pay for the sale to be recorded with the Land Registry (£££). Don't sell that kidney yet! You're nearly over the line! Buyers of properties costing over £ 125,000 (most of them) now have a fortnight to settle stamp duty, a tax paid to the government, although your solicitor will want this from you before exchange of contracts (£££). You're in! As long as the rates have been paid you can celebrate with a nice glass of tap water.

Leasehold

This is an arrangement that means homeowners own the building but not the land it is standing on. If you buy a leasehold flat, you are buying the right to live in the flat for the number of years left on the lease. Once, it was only flats or maisonettes that were sold with fixed-term leases, often lasting hundreds of years, meaning residents had security. On the whole, landlords were benign, charging tiny 'peppercorn' rents and leaving well alone. Moreover, thanks to the 1967 Leasehold Reform Act people were buoyed to know they had the chance to buy that freehold after two years. A slightly convoluted arrangement had been resolved to put all the homeownership eggs in one basket. Sounds good. Until we needed to build a shedload of housing in the 21st century.

For some reason, housebuilders dug up the leasehold idea and started using it in a new and dangerous way: on new-build homes. An estimated 4 million homes in England are leasehold, and it's causing a lot of misery.

Leases come with ground rents and service charges – and not the old fashioned peppercorn rents either, but 'Laika' rents, named after the cosmonaut doggy who sadly went up, but never came down again. Many leaseholds have now become 'fleeceholds', commodities bought and sold by unscrupulous speculators. The worst of this modern breed of lease had the ground rent doubling every ten years, and slapped an inflated price tag on the remainder of the lease, so that residents couldn't buy them outright. Some even charge 'permission fees', to make any changes to the lease, large or small. The whole effect is toxic, with some homeowners becoming prisoners in their own homes, unable to afford spiralling costs and unable to sell because buyers and lenders don't want to get involved in these properties. It needs sorting, and quick.

> *Leaseholds have now become 'fleeceholds', commodities bought and sold by unscrupulous speculators.*

Whatever happens, if you're getting involved in a lease, make sure your solicitor is checking for paragraphs that allow or stipulate a 'Laika' ground rent or service charge.

Here's an example paragraph:

'On each Review Date the Rent is to be increased to double the Rent reserved before the relevant Review Date and the reviewed Rent will be payable from and including the relevant Review Date.'

The government has asked housebuilders to make sure ground rent costs are linked to the rate of inflation, but there's no law in place. So watch your backs!

New builds

The other side of the housebuilding Gold Rush that we've experienced in the past few years is that many homes have been thrown up without due care and attention. I've done loads of stories recently about new-builds that should have been near-perfect on delivery but demonstrated serious flaws with insulation, fire protection and other fundamentals, not to mention the 'snags' – all the little details that should be spot-on when you're buying a new thing. One buyer in Devon reported no fewer than 120 faults in her new home.

Of course, many new homes are committed to off-plan, before they have even been built. The answer should be the NHBC: the New House Builders Council, an organisation that offers a ten-year 'Buildmark' warranty on new homes from a range of big housebuilders. Great idea, but all I'm saying is this: don't pin all your hopes on the NHBC putting things right after the event. They are funded in part by the housebuilders buying these warranties, and so you are not their real customers – the builders are. Many people report the NHBC being of limited use when things go wrong. Check review sites like Trustpilot to see if I'm wrong or if things have changed since I wrote this. In any case, if you have the chance, you're much better off identifying problems before you purchase. Similarly, buying brand new homes off plan gives developers a chance to present an idyllic and persuasive version of your home and its proposed environs. Although they may start out with the best of intentions, as the money gets tighter and the workforce dries up, builders can end up changing elements of a new estate that could make a difference.

> *Check review sites like Trustpilot to see if I'm wrong or if things have changed since I wrote this.*

Play areas, amenities such as shops and surgeries, green spaces, wheelie bin storage and cycle lanes can all go. If you've bought from a plan keep an eye on progress at the site, so that what's delivered matches the promise. Plans for one estate in Devon originally featured a gently sloping diagonal street but during construction this was replaced with steep steps, instantly barring wheelchair users and pram-pushing mums. That's another thing that can transform homes from sanctuaries to jails.

SELLING A HOUSE

Just bought a house? Well, you have now hugely increased the likelihood that you will, one day, have to sell the thing!

Estate agents should be working for you now, as their commission is worked out as a percentage of the sale price. This is typically around 1.5 per cent (plus VAT at 20 per cent of that), but it's ALWAYS Marvin Haggler negotiable, no matter what they say. Suited and booted traditional agents are under huge pressure from online estate agents, who tend to charge a flat fee – a fraction of what the traditional agents willl want. Where they will come in useful – and none of them will thank me for saying this – is giving you a free valuation of your property as part of their sales pitch. Get three of these at the very least before you decide what to do, and use the Land Register price paid site (see p. 212) to see what property around you is doing. Traditional estate agents say their big advantage is the local knowledge they can use to get you the best possible price, and some of the most established ones are certainly justified in claiming that, but they're equally likely to use that knowledge to get themselves the best deal – either by snaffling the best properties cut-price before they ever get to market, or by shifting them for a quick turnaround sale. After all, as we've already said, 1.5 per cent of nothing is nothing.

So what do you lose by going the digital route with an online estate agent? Well, it's more likely you will have to show people around the place in person, for example, which can interfere with your schedule somewhat. Having said that, many now offer a premium hybrid service: a 'local property expert' who may conduct viewings and communicate with buyers, but still for a flat fee that will beat Mr 1.5 per cent. Over the past ten years or so online estate agents have had the same trajectory as tweed waistcoats since *Peaky Blinders* – from something your weird old uncle might do to mainstream and even chic. They won't keep the chill off your kidneys though.

However it's sold, every home that comes onto the market must have an Energy Performance Certificate (EPC), another charge to consider. But if you are a buyer, moving house might give you the opportunity to re-mortgage at a better rate than the one you are on. Even if you can't, there's the possibility of porting your mortgage to the new property, thus cutting costs.

> Over the past ten years or so online estate agents have had the same trajectory as tweed waistcoats since Peaky Blinders.

Removals

Hey, let's stick all our possessions in a van and let some strangers drive it away! What could possibly go wrong?

Unless you own a truck or are part of The A-Team, if you've been living in your own place for a while, you'll need a removal company. It's one of the easiest professions to get involved in, given that the only qualifications required are working limbs, spatial awareness and access to a van. As a result, what you get can vary widely.

In this digital age, check out online reviews and secure a number of quotes. It's well worth getting together with your chosen removal company before the big day to assess what's needed. They are the experts and they should advise you about the size of van and team you will need. Be clear about what you are expecting from them, and what they should expect from you. For example, don't say you will pack up cases yourself then leave half your stuff strewn across the floor. Don't insist on a cheaper small lorry when a bigger one is needed. Conversely, ask how fragile items will be protected and what level of insurance exists. Stories about removal men refusing to unload boxes at their destination until they receive extra payments in cash are legion. Blackmail is never pretty but you are likely to pay up to retrieve personal items. If you end up in dispute there is a non-profit Removals Ombudsman. Pay with a credit card because Section 75

Matt Nav

My mate Stan bought a van and started doing removals. He's a lovely fella, and not a dodgepot in the slightest, but he's up for an adventure and certainly got some amazing stories out of his new career. One of his first jobs was to move an anarchist pirate radio station, under cover of the night, out of their secret bunker in Amsterdam. I don't know how he got paid – possibly in lentils or berets. Another customer arranged pick-up from London, but didn't disclose the destination. Once Stan had loaded the lorry with her worldly possessions, she revealed they were going to Marbella, southern Spain. He drove 40 hours on the road, non-stop, as she poked him and fed him energy drinks. When they arrived she instructed him to leave everything on the lawn. He wasn't even invited in for a glass of water! #roguecustomer (see p. 23) gives you the chance to claim back associated costs if things go wrong – not just the cost of removals themselves.

There are other simple things you can do to alleviate the pain of moving day. Colour-coding boxes to indicate which room they are destined for will help make the off-load a bit less fraught. Don't forget to take meter readings and inform the utility companies you are off. Kettle, cups and a packet of biscuits should be on top of the last box you pack. Why? Because helpers are less restive when they're offered a digestive.

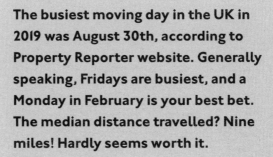

Matt Stat

The busiest moving day in the UK in 2019 was August 30th, according to Property Reporter website. Generally speaking, Fridays are busiest, and a Monday in February is your best bet. The median distance travelled? Nine miles! Hardly seems worth it.

chapter
seven

Bills

Like the tide, every month we see the money come in, and then we watch it go out, but how many of us really understand the bills we pay? On Watchdog, over the years we've found that most of us could be paying a lot less than we are if we really took the time to dig down to find another supplier, or even just threaten to do so. Here's a way to work out where your home is leaking money and how to plug the hole.

ENERGY

There was a time when your electricity and gas were generated, distributed and supplied by one of the area electricity or gas boards. You paid the same price as your neighbour and either waited for the bill to drop on the doormat every quarter or stuck another 50 pence in the meter as and when it was needed. Morecambe and Wise were on the telly, and milk was delivered to the door. It was, in short, a simpler time.

That all changed in 1986 for gas and 1989 for lecky when they were privatised. This cleared the path for dozens of new companies to pipe the power to heat and light our homes. Those companies are keen to attract customers, but as gas and electricity don't really vary in quality they can only really compete on two things: price and customer service. And green-ness, a bit. OK, three things. It's a curious situation which raises a question. When you effectively have the chance to buy the same pair of shoes from 60 different shops, how do you choose where to go?

The companies buy energy at home and overseas at the best possible price – often years ahead in an attempt to beat price hikes – but they're still at the whim of the markets, and as a result, so are our bills. The price of liquefied natural gas (LNG), for example, is in part linked to

> *When you effectively have the chance to buy the same pair of shoes from 60 different shops, how do you choose where to go?*

oil prices, which can rocket skywards if demand is high or supply poor. In short, when demand is high, prices rise, and when it falls, the costs are lowered. Since privatisation the numbers of companies bidding for our energetic affections has blossomed to around 70, although a couple of recent mergers and takeovers mean that number has been scaled back a bit. This still provides us with a bewildering number of choices, all trying to prove that they're different while consistently offering the same pair of shoes. Customer service is a different matter. Some genuinely are better than others, but you won't really know until you become a customer and have the misfortune to have to contact them.

Getting overly familiar with Bill

Considering that every household gets one, energy bills are still remarkably difficult to understand. Electricity bills are written in a language that's peculiar to themselves. Most of us cut to the chase and focus on the big number in the box at the bottom. But understanding what makes up your bill is one of the first steps to cutting that final big number.

Your bill is, like an old-fashioned electric fire, essentially made up of two elements: a standing charge and cost of usage. The standing charge – also known as the fixed charge or daily unit rate – is not to pay for the electricity used, rather the costs of getting it into your home, keeping everything working, meter readings and even government initiatives getting us to use less electricity or more green energy. Some electricity companies are offering deals where the standing charge is set at zero. Sounds great, right? Well, yes, but there is balance in these things. If your standing charge is low or zero, it must follow that the company is making its money somewhere. It's likely that the actual cost of using the electricity will be well ahead of the curve. Horses for courses: if you're in charge of a property that stands empty for large chunks of the year, then this arrangement might make sense.

> One kWh powers a power shower for six minutes or a broadband router for five whole days.

The other bit, the cost of the electricity you use, is charged in units known as kilowatt hours or kWh. Basically, a kWh is the amount of energy that would be used if you kept a 1,000-watt appliance on for an hour. But of course, different appliances use different amounts of lecky. One kWh powers a power shower for six minutes or a broadband router for five whole days. The kWh is the leveller, measured by your meter as its wheels spin round or its LCD digits add up. Gas bills are calculated using cubic metres – the volume of gas used – but then a little calculation has to take place because the power it provides differs slightly depending on where it's sourced, and you end up with, guess what? Kilowatt hours! Just like electricity. Like I said, the great leveller.

Being chased by the Old Bill

So far, so good, except that, until recently, there was still a lot of guesswork involved. Electricity and gas meters would be checked sporadically, and in the time in between inspections billing would rely on estimations of typical use for that household for that time of year. These could be wildly inaccurate, leading to huge discrepancies either way, only to be discovered when a man with an ID badge and a torch asked to look in your garage or under the stairs. Because we're often out when he calls, it costs loads of money to send that man out, and he's an easy thing to cut, the readings sometimes didn't happen for years, leaving householders with a huge debt (or repayment of money they might need) through no fault of their own.

No longer. Back-billing beyond a year previous has been banned by Ofgem. Anything the lecky (or gas) company misses as a result

A recent Uswitch survey found that energy suppliers were amongst the worst for getting bills wrong.

of their error before 12 months ago is yours for free to keep. And it's just as well. A recent Uswitch survey found that energy suppliers were amongst the worst for getting bills wrong. 20 per cent of customers have been billed in error, 11 per cent twice. Loads are still trying it on though, issuing bills for historic use. Don't fall for it: you have Ofgem on your side, and they know karate. Copy them in on any correspondence to give it that extra oomph, and don't forget that switching is the ultimate sanction if your contract is up.

Matt Nav

Because of the scale of their business, when energy companies get it wrong, they can get it all the way wrong. In January 2020 Ovo agreed to pay £8.9 million into a repayment fund after issuing inaccurate or incomplete information to customers. Inaccurate statements were sent to more than 500,000 customers between July 2015 and February 2018, a further 10,000 customers were not warned about tariff renewals while 8,000 people paid over the odds on prepayment deals. Since then the company has invested better in its systems so the same issues don't arise again.

Meters

It's really a good idea to submit your own meter readings regularly. If you see EST on your bill then the figure used is an estimate, and could be all over the place. There are four types of meter: digital, electronic, dial and smart. With the first three, read from left to right, ignoring the final figure which is red, encased in red or follows a decimal point, and dispatch the figure to your supplier. Simples. And then we come to smart meters.

Smart meters are a story all in themselves, and one we've covered loads on *Watchdog*. Talk about a c*ck-up.

In essence, they're a good idea. Smart meters are free to the customer (well, we all share the cost) and a smart meter means an end to a knock on the door from the man with the torch, or, more likely, the card that says you missed him. The meters beam back your reading automatically, for both gas and lecky, meaning you can relax and watch series 23 of *Grey's Anatomy* knowing that is taken care of. You can also, via a little screen, keep an eye on your energy consumption, and marvel as the numbers dip and soar with each boiling of the kettle.

It's no wonder that the energy companies and the government in tandem are so keen for every house to have a smart meter installed. They say that the data compiled about the way that we all use energy will help the industry be smarter in the way it provides homes.

The industry gets to do away with the inefficiency of meter people endlessly knocking on doors, and your bill is, in theory, always accurate. In fact, the government is so keen it has set targets for the industry. Every home and business – that's 51.9 million of them – must be offered one by the end of 2020.

And that's where the problem lies...

Because they're nowhere near that. As I write, there are now just 17 million smart meters in people's homes, and plenty of stories of botched and dangerous installations and negligible savings for households. When the meters don't work, your provider will revert to estimated readings, so we're back where we started. Add to that the bewildering fact that many smart meters can't be switched from one provider to another – in a system that relies on customers doing just that to get the best deal – and you can see why people aren't jumping to be part of the revolution. The date for completion has now been pushed back to 2024, and even that seems hopeful. A new generation of smart meter has been developed: SMETS2. It's claimed it will overcome many of the issues of its predecessor, SMETS 1, by being switchable and more reliable.

> *As I write, there are now just 17 million smart meters in people's homes, and plenty of stories of botched and dangerous installations.*

If you do want to plump for a smartie, definitely make it a SMETS2 to be future proof. Whether you'll get one, though, depends on where you live, and how long you're prepared to wait. Provision is as patchy as a geography teacher's elbow, and there may be huge stocks of SMETS I boxes just sitting on shelves for customers who don't know any better.

Whatever you're told by the call centre, you don't have to have a smart meter. The government has started turning the screws, hinting that anyone with a dumb meter could end up being charged more. Talking of which…

Prepaid energy deals

These are typically installed in properties where there's a poor history of bill payment – even if the current occupiers have always paid up on time. These meters – using a key, a card or tokens – are also sometimes there for the convenience of a landlord who doesn't want the bother of tenants switching bills when they could just hand over a key to be topped up. On the whole, unless things change drastically, if you can avoid paying for your energy this way, you should. Prepaid deals are among the worst tariffs you can get, although many suppliers claim they are getting more competitive. In practice, it means that the communities with the least in their pockets are charged the most for their power. Power, not to the people.

The other side to this is that in shared flats or bedsits with a single meter, it can be really difficult to split the bill between all the occupants. You can have a payment rota, but what if it's Sonia's turn and she's out because Sonia always does Taekwondo on a Tuesday? Are you just going to let the lights go out? Awkward, annoying and divisive. Do whatever you can to get billed retrospectively, and then make sure Sonia kicks butt AND pays her share.

Fuel poverty

The definition of fuel poverty is when a household cannot reasonably keep their home warm, given their income. It's additionally defined as when fuel costs are more than 10 per cent of the household income. As of 2017, more than one in ten households in England were living in fuel poverty – some 2.5 million families. The government's Warm Home Discount Scheme is for anyone on pension credit or a low income and offers a £140 reduction on electricity bills, from participating energy companies.

> *As of 2017, more than one in ten households in England were living in fuel poverty.*

Fuel poverty is more acute still in Scotland. A quarter of homes there fall into that category, and it's those in the north of Scotland who are hardest hit. Not only is it colder there, so homes need more heating, but the cost of electricity distribution is higher because homes are so spread out. In many rural areas there's no gas supply so electricity and oil are the only options. The national green tariff subsidy – standing at 8 per cent – is paid for by electricity customers alone, meaning that if you've only got electric, you're paying for it twice (light and heat), compared to dual fuel households, who pay just once.

Anyone struggling should think about saving money by switching energy provider.

Matt Nav

What's an average user? Hard to predict average usage, given that it's dependent on weather, insulation and so forth, but price comparison site UK Power has come up with some ballpark figures to reflect monthly and annual costs. For a 1–2 bedroom home that has gas and electricity – dual fuel – it's £66 pm/£795 pa, while the figures for a 3–4 bedroom house are £97 pm/£1,163 pa. A gas bill for the smaller place runs out at £33 pm/£396 pa, or £48 pm/£576 pa for the larger one, while in all-electric households it's £34 pm/£408 pa or £49 pm/£588 pa. Don't budget using these figures though. They're so ballpark that they smell of hotdogs.

Switch it up!

Right, simple basic fact: if you haven't switched in a couple of years, the chances are that you're paying too much for your energy. Switching is one of the least liked domestic chores, but unlike unclogging hair from the shower drain, this one could save you hundreds of pounds for ten minutes' work.

Your first stop will be an online comparison site. Steady! Not all of these are created equal, and some actually endorse certain providers, so pick one that reveals all the options available. Ofgem offers an accredited list. The first question you will be asked is where you live. The price of electricity rises and falls by region, depending on whether there are generators nearby, the population density and the costs imposed by the local distribution network (LDN). In case you're interested, the East Midlands enjoys the cheapest fuel bills in the country. Let's all move to Derby! To get the best results, you then need to know how much electricity you are likely to use. If you haven't got access to an exact amount, an educated guess is better

Matt Stat

According to Uswitch, switching saved £1.7 billion pounds on British bills in 2019. That could be you! Not the whole 1.7 billion. It's not the National Lottery.

than sticking with an over-priced tariff. The comparison site will regurgitate the tariffs on offer and, while they all have different bells and whistles, they should sound and look something like this:

→ **Standard variable tariff**: With prices that can rise and fall with the market, it is flexible and it won't have a fee for leaving – but nor is it likely to be the cheapest available. People may find themselves demoted to this when another headline deal has come to an end. Unless you're Braveheart and value your freedom so much that you're prepared to paint yourself blue, you need to move on from this one pronto. You're paying too much.

← **Fixed energy tariff:** This has a price guarantee until an agreed date. But if you want to leave before that to take advantage of cheaper prices elsewhere there will probably be a charge, unless the end of the agreement is only a matter of eight weeks or less away.

→ **Dual fuel tariff:** Getting gas and electricity from the same provider can be cheaper and easier, but beware convenience isn't coming at a price and that two separate tariffs wouldn't be better value. Still compare individual deals to see if you can do better.

← **Online energy tariff:** Go paper free, save a tree and 20p. Not massive savings, but hey, it's not just about money, is it? Talking of which…

→ **'Green' tariff:** The supplier promises to match your usage with energy generated from renewable sources or offset it by backing environmental projects. Britain clocked up its first coal-free fortnight of a generation in May 2019, in the same year that solar power levels hit new records. It all sounds great but your principles could cost you. The flipside is that your custom shows that there is demand to use more renewables, and will drive change.

← **Pre-payment tariff:** See p. 237.

→ **'Time of Use' tariff:** Suitable for those who use electricity when demand is low. Enjoy a cup of coffee while you're doing the ironing at 3am? You're in luck! We have just the tariff for you!

OK, it's clear that our headline here is about getting you the best deal, but as in all things, if you make a judgement just based on price, you may come a proper cropper. We've seen loads of smaller providers offer blistering deals, only to find out pretty soon that they haven't got the personnel or systems to handle the custom they've generated. The phrase they always use is 'victims of our own success' but like Marmite on a fur coat, that just doesn't wash. If you're going to promise something, deliver, or don't waste my time sitting on your phone line listening to 'Greensleeves' again. Ask yourself: has this firm been bubbling away for a while like a casserole? Or are they more of a crepe suzette – a disruptive flash in the pan then they're gone?

Matt Nav

Still in the dark about the company providing your lights? Suppliers are required by Ofgem to provide figures about the number of complaints they receive per 100,000 customers as a point of comparison. They also have to supply their top five reasons for complaints, and show their working about what they are doing to improve the situation. It's all good stuff if you want to put the price you're paying into context. It also shows that complaints across the board have dropped substantially in the last ten years, presumably because of the efforts of all of us here on *Watchdog*. Yes, I'm pretty confident that's the reason.

After you've made your decision and confirmed the switch there's a cooling off period (see CCR, p. 19) in case you change your mind. But after 17 days the two electricity companies involved in the switch will make the appropriate arrangements. Don't worry, you won't notice a thing. The lights won't flicker and you won't miss *Match of the Day*. It should be seamless (see the section on the supplier of last resort, p. 245). You should just get a welcome pack through the post that will indicate the change has been made. Switch and switch often. You can change suppliers a dozen times a year if the right deals are there – but watch out for termination charges.

If the price cap fit

Shocking stat: despite all the above advice, 54 per cent of us – 11 million households – are marooned on the standard variable rate, throwing money down the road like it doesn't matter. For those people there's a degree of protection offered by the fuel price cap, working since January 2019 and set by Ofgem. This doesn't mean a cap on your overall bill, because life just doesn't work like that. The cap is on the price per unit – per kWh. If you use lots, your bill will rise correspondingly. The cap – which also varies by region – only applies to those who use a prepayment meter, get the government's Warm Home Discount or are on a 'standard variable' energy tariff. The aim is to protect those who aren't adept at switching. Ofgem sets the levels of the caps twice a year, in February and August, and these peg the unit price. The level of the cap rises or falls, depending on how much the providers are paying on the international energy market. If there's a fall in costs, the cap should ensure it is passed on to customers. This is exactly what happened in August 2019, when maximum prices were driven down. Meanwhile, suppliers are protected from being handcuffed to cheap deals in the face of steep wholesale rises. But, Ofgem warn, the tariffs linked to the price cap are not necessarily the cheapest and you are almost certainly still better off making a switch. There's a theme emerging here...

> *Seven out of ten homes are supplied by what's known as 'the big six'.*

Seven out of ten homes are supplied by what's known as 'the big six' energy companies: British Gas, EDF Energy, E.On, npower, ScottishPower and SSE. The price cap has helped to dispel fears about any price fixing among those who dominate the market. But when consumers depend on competition to drive down prices, all big fish make the pond seem smaller.

The supplier of last resort

More than a dozen of the minnows in the energy supply business have gone bust since 2018. Thankfully, customers aren't plunged into darkness, as their accounts are transferred by Ofgem to what's known as 'a supplier of last resort' (SoLR). If a firm goes out of business its customers are effectively auctioned to participating companies by Ofgem, usually within a matter of days. The switch is intended to be seamless. It isn't always. We've seen customers whose account credit and payments have been lost in translation with these swap-overs. If your provider goes belly up, treat it like a house move. Take meter readings, keep statements, get screengrabs of online accounts – anything you can do to prove your point if your new provider develops a blank expression.

Above all, look for the best deal by switching.

Are you getting the message? Switch it up, people!

Matt Nav

Don't switch! What? Matt! You just told us all to switch! You're twisting my melon, man!

OK, yes, I'll admit this is a bit of a curveball, but let me tell you about the virtual switch. It's a Marvin Haggler Masterclass that gives you all the savings of switching, with a fraction of the hassle. Start like a switch, but then take all the info you've gathered from shopping around for a better deal, stick it on a piece of paper and call up your current provider, ready for a bit of a ding dong. Tell them you're leaving, that your bags are packed and you're ready to go. They will send you through to their retention or cancellation department, who have a special role: to keep you on board. Big companies spend millions attracting new customers in highly competitive markets like energy and phones. Once they've got you they don't want to lose you. The departments are authorised to offer you much better deals to get you to turn around and unpack that valise.

We did this a couple of years ago on *Watchdog*, and the results were astounding. Most of the participants saved hundreds. The most successful saved £1,100, meaning she could fly to the States on holiday. And she didn't have to change a thing!

Stay loyal and live like a royal!

Direct debits

Paying your energy bills by direct debit could save you cash each year, and that's a good thing. But issues linked to direct debits have given switching a bad rep. Sometimes the cost is higher than you thought it would be because the amount you pay is set by suppliers. Fine if their estimate about your annual usage is spot on. Not so great if it's overestimated and you end up paying more than you need to each month. Sometimes, people have made the switch hoping to save on their bills, only to see their monthly payments rise sharply, as the new provider ups the usage estimate. Of course, any extra money will end up appearing as credit on the bill but trying to get that back can be a bit of a saga. You're better off with the money in your account.

Underpayment works the same way, but with a hefty bill at the end of the year. I've switched a couple of times only to find that what I end up paying is nothing like what I was quoted. It's not a reason not to bother – just keep your eyes open. If you do fall into debt, talk to your provider as soon as possible, as they have options, with most overseeing an energy fund for those who have fallen into hardship. You could find yourself with a payment plan or a prepaid meter, so best not, eh?

Power cuts

Being abruptly plunged into darkness during a power cut isn't any fun. The good news is you are entitled to modest compo if it happens. If the blackout lasts for more than 12 hours in normal weather the rates are £75 for every domestic customer and £150 for businesses. A further £35 is due for every subsequent 12-hour period. You can also claim £75 if you are cut off more than four times a year, for three hours or more on each occasion. Following bad weather the connection companies have more leeway but householders are entitled to £70 after being 24 hours off grid in the wake of a category 1 storm. For the worst weather, the companies are permitted 48 hours to reinstate power before compensation kicks in. As long as you can find your phone in the dark…

WATER BILLS

We take clean water gushing out of our taps for granted, but it's an expensive business, keeping the water crystal clear, and that's reflected in our bills.

Costs vary around the regions. As with electricity, the national water board was privatised in 1989 but here there are just 32 companies in the business. There's no switching option with water. It's the local company that gets the gig, although you might receive water from one company while another deals with your sewage. Thus the bill is either joint or comes in two parts: the first for tap water coming in and the second for waste water (rain and sewage) heading out of the household.

To some, it seems like the water companies have got it easy. After all, water falls freely from the sky.

To some, it seems like the water companies have got it easy. After all, water falls freely from the sky. But you're not paying just for good quality water but also for reservoirs, pumping stations, sewer pipes, treatment works, water storage and distribution. Still, the average bill for both parts comes in at £415 per year, according to Discover Water, or just 1.13 pence per day. For every two litres out of your tap at home you are paying about one third of a penny. In a supermarket that water will cost you 45 pence – 90 pence if it's from France and models drink it. So it's a bit of a bargain.

With no competition among companies to force down price, it's up to Ofwat, the economic regulator for the industry, to keep an eagle eye on charges. For some households, having a water meter installed is one way to cut costs. This measures precisely the amount of water that's come out of your taps and charges you accordingly, alongside a fixed standing charge. In general terms, homes with few occupants and economical use of water are better off getting a meter. It can also be a first early warning sign if you've sprung a leak. But not every house is suitable for meter installation, depending on the way their pipes run. If you've been turned down for a meter you can ask for an assessed charge, rooted in the size of your house, the number of people in it and the average bills in your area, which may reduce your costs. Otherwise homes receive a bill that's linked to rateable value instead. If the house is crammed full of people who bathe twice daily, it would be better to steer clear of the meter or the assessed charge. What? You can have as much water as you want? For a fixed annual charge? It turns out that life DOES work that way!

Another way of slashing the waste water side of the bill is to have a soakaway installed. That means digging a hole in the ground in which rainwater will collect, to drain away naturally into the ground. You may have one and not know it. If you have, check that your bill has been reduced accordingly. If you haven't, then it's probably not worth bothering. It will take a long time to make back what you've spent on having it dug.

Billing agents are a bit new to the world of water, and, from what I can see, a bit pointless. They may contact you saying that they can save you money on your water bill by making representations to your water company. Here's all you need to know: Ofwat don't endorse them. They don't do anything you can't do yourself. They're clearly not doing it for nothing. Classic meaningless middle man operation, case closed.

Clean water is not expensive, but it certainly is precious, taking up resources to collect, purify and distribute. However you are billed, there are lots of ways to save water: showering instead of having a bath, turning off the tap while you clean your teeth, only using the washing machine when it's full, popping a water-saving device in the toilet system – often called a hippo – to reduce the number of litres in every flush.

COUNCIL TAX

Who pays for rubbish collections, roads, libraries and leisure centres, parks and public transport? Well, you do, via the council tax, which funnels cash to local authorities so they can lay on literally scores of public services. Known by numerous names down the years, including the rates and the poll tax, the amount of your council tax bill is determined by the size, location and character of your home, as each one falls into a pre-set band linked to its value. Although sometimes the format is slightly tweaked, this property tax is levied in much the same way in every country in the UK. It's an annual bill usually paid in ten instalments.

But the method for evaluating homes and sticking them in bands has been notoriously slapdash in the past. The original valuations for council tax took place in 1991, in a process nicknamed 'second gear valuation', suggesting that the valuers made their banding judgements without stopping their cars. In any case, I certainly look different from how I did in 1991, and no doubt your home and the area it's in also do. Getting a re-evaluation of your home is well worthwhile if you think it's been over-pegged, particularly if it's in one of the top bands and can't go up any more. It could save you hundreds every year, and can even be backdated to correct the error. We're talking a cash sum, ladies and gents, and that doesn't come along all that often.

You'll need to apply to the Valuation Office Agency of England and Wales (Scotland and Northern Ireland, you've got your own thing going on) to get the ball rolling, but a warning: valuations can also put you in a higher band, with bigger bills.

Anyone who lives alone gets a 25 per cent reduction on their council tax, while for students there's no charge at all. Diplomats, carers and anyone aged under 18 are among also among those who don't have to pay. If you think you are entitled to a reduction, contact your local council.

The method for evaluating homes and sticking them in bands is notoriously slapdash.

HOME INSURANCE

The house you live in and the things inside it need insuring every year, in case of fire, flood or toddlers. Buildings insurance, which covers everything fixed in the house like windows, doors and kitchen sinks, is mandatory but it only falls to you if you own the freehold. Renters, that's 100 per cent a landlord cost. If you do own the house, don't get sucked into insuring up to the market value of your home. Many people start throwing money about here but you are only looking to cover the cost of rebuilding the property if disaster strikes, because it's often the location of your place that accelerates the market value. That plot will still be yours, and there's only so much damage you can do to mud.

Keep home maintenance up to scratch as an insurer will see a long-term issue – like a missing slate – as a fine reason not to pay your claim for a new roof. If your circumstances change and you take in a lodger or start a business at home, don't forget to let the insurance company know.

When it comes to contents most people are overly cautious, looking to save a tenner or two in the hope that accidents won't happen. You may think your home contents don't amount to more than £25,000 but it's incredible how it adds up. Replacing tech, carpets and jewellery

> *If you do own the house, don't get sucked into insuring up to the market value of your home.*

will get you there pretty quickly. If you want to claim on a damaged carpet after a burst pipe that's no fault of your own and an assessor sees your home contents are chronically underinsured, he or she will cut the figure so it reflects the level of underpayment. Always work on the basis that you'll be in a battle with your insurer when it comes to paying out on a claim, and give them no excuses not to pay out. These people may help you. That does not make them friends.

Renters are only after insurance for contents. Home owners, on the other hand, can opt for a building/contents combo that places all the eggs in one basket, and usually offers a discount, which may or may not be cheaper than buying both bits individually. Whatever happens, stay smart, shop around whenever renewal comes around, and know that there are hundreds of pounds to be saved whenever your policy has its birthday. Home insurance has actually come down over the last few years, so if you haven't switched, you're probably paying too much. Let's do it!

Have a gander at the price comparison websites, at least three, for the insurance that suits you best. Be blind to the sponsored deals that appear at the top, though. These are in effect advertisements which help pay for the site. If there's an eye-catching quote that's substantially lower than the rest, be sure there are no hidden costs and that it is what you need.

After that, go to the companies that don't appear on price comparison websites (Aviva and Direct Line, for example) to see if they can beat the best quoted price – in the red corner, Marvin Haggler! Sometimes the telephone operators you are talking to are permitted to offer discounts that you won't know about if you don't ask. Always be prepared to walk away. If you've got a hard-to-insure property, like one that suffers from flooding, consult an insurance broker. They'll know who specialises in what you've got.

When looking at policies, remember that they are as individual as snowflakes, and only a thorough reading means you know what you're paying for. Policies usually cover damage from storms, flooding, earthquakes, fire, lightning, vandalism, riots, theft and explosions. Crucially, they should also help if there's subsidence, which means your property starts goes on the wonk as the ground beneath it shifts. But optional items include accidental

> *Policies usually cover damage from storms, flooding, earthquakes, fire, lightning, vandalism, riots, theft and explosions.*

damage, wear and tear, terrorism or if your house has been empty for a bit. Insurers are unlikely to pay for high-value items that you have failed to declare. Some will offer to replace damaged goods with new items, while others only consider 'like for like', i.e. the cost of a used item.

It's also important not to over-insure. Unless you're across all the additional elements of your insurance, you can be paying for cover several times for the same risk. Take a mobile phone away for a holiday in the UK, and you could have travel, home and phone insurance as well as a packaged bank account all covering you if it gets stolen.

Home insurers are really nerdy about locks. You can help yourself to find the best home insurance by fitting grade A locks on windows and doors, with a five-lever mortice deadlock conforming to British Standard 3621 generally perceived as the best of the best. Lesser locks will cost you as much money, and may invalidate a claim if you haven't properly declared them. Don't forget insurers will only pay out for burglaries after a sign of forced entry. That applies to homeowners and those occupying a single room of an HMO. Indeed, while the value of the contents is often low, the risks of shared accommodation are perceived as far greater and it can be more difficult to get contents insurance. Students, check to see if you are covered by the family home's policy, as that remains your permanent address. And that cereal bowl has been there for a month. Clear it up!

chapter
eight

Looking After Your Home

Your precious home, your biggest investment, and the ship in which you sail through life, is a kit of parts. Some of those parts, bricks for instance, seem simple and easy to understand. Other bits, like the insides of your gas boiler, are complex and, unless you're a professional, they should never be tinkered with, even after a couple of glasses of wine.

We may know a bit about roofs or decorating, but none of us is an expert in every aspect of our home. There are just too many components. Similarly, to write about every detail of every part of your home here would require several books, or a series of magazines which you collect month by month. You could spend a lifetime getting to know everything you need to know about your home, by which time you'd be in care. Eventually, we all need to trust someone to do some work for us, and while the vast majority of traders, in my experience, are decent, honest and on the side of the angels, there are a few who have kept me in work for the last 20 years. I'd like to take this opportunity to thank them personally, and to advise you to avoid them like bubonic plague.

So here I'm going to give you a few of the very basics about your pad, and crucially, the most common ways that dodgepot rogue traders will try to be like your mum on your birthday when she knitted that balaclava for you, i.e. pull the wool over your eyes.

Let's start at the bottom and work our way up.

DRAINS

You know they're there, I know they're there, but let's face it, we don't want to deal with them unless we have no other option. Drain rogues know that they're onto a winner because most householders don't have a clue how things get from their sink or toilet to the seaside, and are quite happy to keep it that way.

The solution to most drain problems however, is remarkably simple. The vast majority can be cleared by one experienced operative using a set of connecting polypropylene and brass rods with various attachments at the end. So how many times have I seen sewer rats trying to convince our stooges that the only way to clear the blockage was this sequence?

→ A team of at least two, working together at an extortionate half-hourly rate. Then...

← A jet washing device, which, despite being part of the kit carried on board their van, had to be hired out at an additional half-hourly rate.

→ When this fails, a CCTV camera kit which would identify the location of the blockage. Additional half-hourly rate applies.

← Physical excavation of said drain to mend a crack in the drain which is clearly where all the truth and honesty is leaking out. 'Victorians, you see? Brilliant engineers but these pipes have had their day.'

→ Plus VAT. Despite explicitly asking for a cash payment.

You can see how a minimum call-out charge of 50 or 60 quid can be catapulted during a torturous afternoon into a bill of several hundreds, or even the low thousands. Drains are relatively simple: long tubes of ceramic or plastic that can put up with a lot of unmentionables. If your drain oppo hasn't spent at least the first half hour using a set of the ol' Rod Stewarts to shift the blockage, then odds on he's a chancer who Maggie May be about to rip you off. If they don't allow you to watch them at work, then you should be saying sayonara. If you're on my turf, I need to check your working.

Many blocked drains happen way before the manhole cover in your garden or drive, by which time the diameter of the pipes tends to be larger and straighter. Before you call anyone out, you may want to stick a bucket under the kitchen sink and remove the u-bend. You can also try all sorts of science fair projects with baking soda and white vinegar if that takes your fancy. There are loads of instructional videos on YouTube. People seem to love making that stuff.

Matt Nav

For the pilot episode of *Rogue Traders* we borrowed a house in West London and blocked the drain. We then called out a guy we suspected of stringing jobs out in pretty much the way I've just described. He wouldn't let the householder watch him at work, claiming that the water was splashing everywhere and could be toxic. We had secret cameras on him anyway, so no problem. When he got to the bit where he was supposed to be using CCTV to inspect our drains, we noticed a problem. There was no sign of a CCTV kit on his van. When he was claiming to inspect our drains, he was actually sticking the hose of a carpet cleaner down the manhole opening and shouting, 'I can't see anything! It's a total mystery!' to our stooge. He spent hours doing this and then handed us a gargantuan bill. We later called him out to clean our carpets with the same machine, at which point I stepped out.

'How do you get a picture on this then?' I asked… and two decades of being a smart alec had begun.

DRIVEWAYS

The little road into your house is also, in the wrong hands, a dual carriageway to the contents of your wallet. Unlike drains rogues, the approach is often classic OOTBNFY (see p. 33). Rather than you calling a number of firms from a trusted source to give you a quote, you may get a knock at the door from a friendly face in hi-vis.

What a coincidence! Did you know that they were working down the road for the council, and had a little bit of tarmac/block paving/concrete left over that's just about the size of your drive? How lucky! (This also works for roofs, see p. 281.) They can get started right away. The boys are there, waiting in the van until they get the thumbs up, then it's all hands to the pump, in a whirlwind of activity. Before you know it, your old drive (bit tatty, but basically OK) has gone and a new one is down, blacker and shinier than the morning dew on a raven's wing (if it's tarmac).

The thing is, laying a drive of any kind is like making sushi. It may appear to be simple in execution, but preparation is everything. The constant motion of a heavy car to and fro over a drive means that it must be stable and supported in depth, not just on the surface, if it is to be durable. For instance, a tarmac drive needs to be dug out to allow a membrane to be put down to stop weeds growing

through,
then allow
150mm of
hardcore,

> *I've witnessed gangs who change their tune from happy-go-lucky to menacing at the end of the job in order to pressure customers.*

followed by 50mm of rough tarmac, and finally 20mm of finishing tarmac on top. At each stage this has to be compressed and rolled to make sure the whole thing is even stevens and won't shift once it's put to the test by a Vauxhall Insignia. This is hard work. It needs planning. It can't be carried out at the tail end of a working day just because someone has a bit of blacktop left on the van, and in any case, my friends, that was a great big lie, if you hadn't guessed it. I'm shocked, I tell you! Shocked!

The worst thing about a whirlwind driveway of this sort is not that it will fall apart when the first frost comes. It's the fact it opens the door to aggressive and intimidating negotiating after the event. I've witnessed gangs who change their tune from happy-go-lucky to menacing at the end of the job in order to pressure customers into handing over multiples of the agreed price. They're at your house, and they're not going away until you pay up. Your kids are about to come home from school. So what are you going to do?

OOTBNFY! Jobs like this aren't a spur-of-the moment thing. There is a right way to approach something that will cost you any more than a couple of hundred quid. I've stuck it at the end of this chapter.

GARDENS AND TREES

While we're at ground level, that same gang who just knocked on your door to sort your drive are now wearing chainsaw trousers and have noticed that you have trees or bushes and that they were doing some work for the council, etc., etc.

Garden rogues and fake tree surgeons often work by leafleting an area intensively and harvesting the work it brings over the next few days. This gives them a couple of advantages. Firstly, it makes it hard for enforcement agencies to pin them down. By the time the word has got out that the dodgepots are in town, they've moved on to the next council area. Also, if they receive a call from outside the area, they'll be suspicious that it might be Trading Standards, the police, or an idiot off the telly (investigative consumer journalist). The leaflet gives them complete control of their customer base, and a geographical area of least risk to work within. As far as you're concerned, a leaflet through the door is classic OOTBNFY and a good reason to let your neighbours know that for a couple of weeks at least, you're all residents of Dodgepot City. Watch out for vans with chippers attached. Don't answer the door to them.

Matt Nav

That last bit might sound extreme but I promise you it's not an overreaction. Garden rogues have a really nasty habit of also being distraction burglars. I take as my example a gang based in Essex and Kent who I've met four or five times. Targeting older customers with a pensioner discount (nonsense), they would turn up and start work, accompanied by a 'man from the council' (also a member of their gang). His role was twofold: firstly to convince the householder that due to the need to protect the environment, the green waste their job was generating now attracted a cost for disposal. This pushed the job into many thousands of pounds. Talk about jumping on a news bandwagon! His secondary role was much less Greta Thunberg. While one of the other gang members distracted the householder, he would rifle through drawers and cupboards, even going upstairs into bedrooms to look for jewellery. Their utter contempt for their prey is unbelievable. A lot of this gang is in prison right now, but they'll be out before long, and others will be trying the same, so watch yourselves.

Many real tree surgeons are locally based, and many need a nice bit of land or a yard in which to store equipment, vehicles, logs and the like. You might even find one attached to the local farm or big manor house. It makes it a lot harder for them to do a runner after they've ruined your garden and your savings. Look for cross-checked accreditation by bodies like the Arboricultural Association. Again, ask yourself what they have to lose if the job goes wrong. Not a solid guide, but don't bother with anyone who isn't wearing the right protective clothing. If they can't be bothered to protect themselves from a chainsaw, they aren't going to worry about anything else, particularly doing your job right.

> *Ask yourself what they have to lose if the job goes wrong.*

EXTERIOR WALLS AND DAMP-PROOFING

One of the loveliest things I've ever done on Rogue Traders is sit and spend time with expert surveyor Barry Cross as he drips water onto a house brick. He does this not to torture the brick into giving up its secrets, but to prove a simple point. Bricks absorb water. They are meant to. It's a design feature. They get wet. They dry out. And nobody gets hurt.

However, there is an entire industry set up to convince you that this is a bad thing. Two, in fact. The first is a pressure sales industry that will tell you your bricks need a coating on the outside which makes water run off, and which may also give your house a thermal coating that could save you money on your heating bills. The name of this incredible product is: Hogwash. Apply a coat of hogwash to your walls and magically you will see thousands of

> *Apply a coat of hogwash to your walls and magically you will see thousands of pounds evaporate.*

pounds evaporate from your account. They will advertise this service by offering an OOTBNFY free, no-obligation survey* which requires someone to come round your house and break a fair number of the CPFUTR 2008 (p. 16) while sitting on your sofa and drinking your tea.

Damp-proofing is a bit different. There's a good chance that this comes not entirely OOTBNFY. It may even have been prompted by the survey of your house by a chartered surveyor which took place before you bought the thing. A terrible admission coming right now:

This happened to me.

A survey of our first flat revealed that we had rising damp. This could be resolved, said our friendly surveyor, if we had an injection of a silicon liquid into the walls. Luckily enough, he knew just the firm. Our flat was stripped of plaster in the bedroom and hall, and a team came in to do the work of injecting a chemical at pressure into the bottom of our walls, at a cost of over a thousand pounds in old money (1998). Sitting in the living room, as the first layer of plaster came off, I distinctly heard one of the guys say, 'This has already been done.' We'd been had. I sat down and didn't say anything until they'd finished and left. It was the last time I ever did that.

---

* Not free. Obligations apply. Not a survey.

Matt Nav

Damp-proofing is such a lucrative scam that it's attracted a proper criminal element in some parts. Back in the noughties, we investigated a damp-proofing boss who funded homes in Florida and Portugal by sending out a number of teams to con the elderly in the North West of England. He laundered money, travelled between his homes on fake passports and threatened anyone who tried to compete with his business. This got really nasty. On one occasion he kept a rival in the basement of his villa in the Algarve with his feet in a bucket of petrol, threatening to light it if he didn't take his finger out of the dodgy damp-proofing pie. If that were me, I'd hot foot it out of the place and never look back.

Bricks take in water, just like Barry Cross showed me. To stop water going up walls – in itself a matter of debate – most houses have a damp-proof course: a layer of slate or bitumen felt a few courses up which stops water going any further. Selling damp-proofing sometimes means persuading the householder that this damp-proof course (DPC) has been breached. Think about it. How did this happen? Shifting of the tectonic plates? It's very unlikely. Whatever the science behind it, a huge chunk of the damp-proofing industry is a lasting con that just won't go away, playing on our fears of structural damage to our biggest investment. Damp in homes is often from other, completely unrelated sources, like a broken guttering system, broken windows or poor drainage. Squeezing stuff into or slapping stuff onto brick walls is rarely the answer. I'm also not entirely convinced that there wasn't some sort of reciprocal arrangement going on between my surveyor and the damp-proofing company. I've read many similar stories since. Ah, well. If you're going to make your mistakes, make 'em early!

LOCKS

Let's go through the front door! Locks. Such a small thing. Such a great way to lose money to dodgepots. This is because when you need work on your locks you are usually:

→ desperate to get back in to your house and therefore

← without the time or means to source a reputable person to sort it.

That's when you end up calling the first dodgy locksmith you can find, who will drill out your lock, fit a new one and charge you like a wounded rhino for the privilege. Proper locksmiths don't drill unless they've run out of other options. They pick or slip, leaving your lock intact and saving you time and money. Just like rods for the legit drain guy, the real locksmith carries and uses his picks with pride, and you should accept no substitute. For reasons I'll detail later on, I don't like recommending trade bodies and federations, but I make an exception for the excellent Master Locksmiths Association who guard their knowledge jealously and tend not to admit muppets. I'd make them your first stop lock shop. Right, we're in the hall. Hey! The radiators aren't on! It's freezing!

GAS FITTING AND PLUMBING

Well now, what have we here? A veritable cornucopia of roguery! Certainly, if you were to go over the last couple of decades of Rogue Traders you would come to the conclusion that plumbers are nothing but a bunch of blackguards and scoundrels, who are looking to divert a pipeline full of cash into their own pockets.

The opposite is true. The vast majority of plumbers work hard for their money, have a difficult and sometimes dirty job, and are decent and honest. We only go looking for the bad ones to show you what they get up to and how you can avoid it. There are a few, and the damage they can do is really shocking.

Please note the distinction I make between gas fitting and plumbing. As a shorthand, think boilers vs toilets. A gas fitter needs to be, in some sense, a plumber. A plumber doesn't necessarily need to be a gas fitter. It's not just in a name; it's a legal difference. To work on gas – specifically, to interrupt the gas supply and work legally and safely on gas appliances – your fitter must be registered with an organisation called Gas Safe. This involves training, approval and accreditation that take time and money. It's a big commitment, but worth it to ensure that when they

> *A plumber doesn't necessarily need to be a gas fitter. It's not just in a name; it's a legal difference.*

leave, you're safe from gas leaks, explosions and carbon monoxide poisoning. We're not mucking about here. We have seen plenty of rogues who try to steer round this question by offering someone else's number, or that of the firm, or even by faking their Gas Safe cards. Get their GS number before they start work and – crucially – check back with Gas Safe that they are who they say they are. If the picture looks like Danny DeVito, but the guy in front of you has a shock of ginger hair, make your excuses and get him away from your boiler.

If there's something wrong with your heating system then it will need a diagnosis. Make sure that you get the diagnosis and a firm quote before any work starts. If a part has failed, try to find that part with local suppliers, and get a price. This means you'll have a good idea if you're being charged 400 per cent mark-up as a way to build the job. Also, gas fitters and plumbers charge by the hour or half hour, so a two-hour trip to a parts supplier through traffic can send your bill through the roof. Showing your fitter where they can find one nearby takes this temptation out of their hands. Make sure you see receipts for any parts bought and get the old part in your hands after the job is done.

Get a key (pennies) and unlock the secret to quieter, more efficient heating.

Here is a gift for you. Got a combi boiler? The most common problem it's going to have is a drop in pressure. You'll have no hot water until it's back up, but you can do it yourself and it's really easy. There are two water inlet pipes under the boiler. They'll probably have tap handles. There should be a pressure gauge on the front of the boiler. Opening both of these valves will let water in, building the pressure. Don't go at it like a bull at a gate. Let it gently increase until you get somewhere between 1 and 1.5. Then stop. If your boiler isn't filling a steaming bath and giving you hot showers, or if it keeps dropping pressure again, then you may have a leak. In that case, call someone out. If you've sorted the problem then pour a small drink and toast me heartily, for I have saved you time and money and you are once again bodily clean. Similarly, if you have gas central heating but you don't know how to bleed your radiators, you're asking for someone to come over and charge you like a rugby league player. Get a key (pennies) and unlock the secret to quieter, more efficient heating.

Ballcocks and washers

Now we're properly on to the plumbing side of things: ballcocks and taps. Good news for you, but a problem for rogue plumbers, is that it's quite hard to make a big job out of the most common things that go wrong. Toilets and taps are quite simple, and the two main things that might happen are some sort of leaky or sticky problem with your ballcock valve, and a washer failing on your tap, causing it to leak or not turn fully. Both of these are fiddly, but ultimately not expensive or terribly time-consuming.

A ballcock is a device that uses an air-filled float (usually spherical, often orange) to shut off a valve when the water in your toilet or cold water cistern reaches a certain level. I've found a beautiful brass one online for £70, but usually you'll be paying something like £30 top whack. They do take a little while to fit, but you should be all sorted in an hour or so. Modern loos swap the ballcock for a cartridge system to save space. It's still straightforward to fix but might be a bit harder to find exactly the right one.

When taps drip it's usually because the little plastic or rubber washers inside have failed. These aren't specialist parts, they cost pennies, and most plumbers should have them. At the very worst, they'll have to replace the taps, for instance, if the valve seating is damaged. In either case, if your plumber is still in the house after an hour, it's either because they've had a seizure or because they want to find out what's for dinner. Either call for an ambulance or a takeaway.

ELECTRICS

OK! Electrics! Definitely not to be mixed with water. By electrics I mean anything that is part of the system supplying mains electricity to your home, after the meter. The meter and anything before it (going out to the street) is the responsibility of UK Power Networks, and that's who you need to contact if there's a problem.

Coming out of the meter you'll see a pair of wires (tails) which go into a board with a load of flicky switches on it, typically black or red. Your dad might have once called these fuses, on a fuseboard. But not any more. If they were fitted at any point since the *Back to the Future* film franchise, they're likely to be residual current devices (RCDs), and that box they're in is a consumer unit, so please call it that or face ridicule. RCDs are magical, life-saving little gizmos which sense if current is leaking from the circuit, and switch themselves off immediately, reducing the risk to anyone or anything into which that current may be flowing. They're also a clear indication that something may be wrong with your electrics somewhere, and since

> *RCDs are magical, life-saving little gizmos which sense if current is leaking from the circuit.*

2008 electricians working on your house have to make sure all your sockets are protected by one. It's really worth spending just a little time getting to know your consumer unit. I'm not saying you should buy it lunch, but you should definitely work out which RCD switch turns which lights and sockets on and off. This is a two-person job, and requires a lot of shouting upstairs and resetting of clocks, but buying a set of sticky labels means you'll only have to do it once. Probably also worth waiting until the washing machine has finished its cycle.

Identifying and labelling your RCDs also gives you a headstart when identifying any electrical problems that occur in your house. A tripped RCD means one or a few sockets or lights are leaking electricity, and isolating which one means you don't have to shut down the whole house just to be safe. It also means that when and if you do have to call out an electrician, they are less likely to stitch you up like a kipper. A very common scam is to needlessly upgrade the whole consumer unit at a cost of around £500. Electrical safety standards are constantly being upgraded, and if your electrician is dodgy they'll use that as an excuse to replace things that were working perfectly well.

Electricians, like gas fitters, can't just wake up one morning and decide that's what they are today. They have to qualify to a level where their work conforms to Part P of the Building Regulations which govern everything we live and work in. This is designed to keep us safe from shocks and fires. Typically, electricians will have passed a vocational qualification and then registered with one of the bodies that oversees Part P, like the NICEIC, although that isn't a legal requirement. What it gives you, as a customer, is a backstop which shows they have put the hours in, get regularly assessed and, crucially, have something at risk if it all goes wrong. Registered electricians also have to have public liability insurance, another handy safeguard if your Christmas guests start getting fritzed by your fridge. It's the sort of thing dodgepot electricians won't bother with, and you'll forget to ask about, in your desperation to get the lights back on.

Right. The lights are typically above your head, in the ceiling, and that means there is only one place left to go.

ROOFS, GUTTERS AND CHIMNEYS

It's all up there! Above our heads, keeping us dry, are the various bits of ceramic, steel and plastic that keep a house waterproof and windproof, taking smoke up and out and water down and away. And yet it's a world of mystery. We rarely look up at our roofs, let alone get up a ladder to have a look, which makes it a fertile playground for a range of dodgepots, working at altitude with an attitude.

We've already talked about our OOTBNFY gang, and seen them change from their sticky tarmac slacks into chainsaw trousers to persuade you they're tree surgeons. Well, now those same goons have got their ladders out, and are knocking on your door because they're in the area and couldn't help noticing that some of your roof tiles have slipped. Letting these roof monkeys loose is opening the door to a world of pain, because if there weren't problems with your roof before, there certainly will be now. Suddenly, to that slipped tile you can add a chimney pot that needs re-pointing, ridge tiles that need lifting and re-seating, gutters that need replacing, rotten soffit boards, new felt for the flat roof and even a special treatment that will seal your roof forever against the wet and the cold.

What's this? You have squirrels nesting in your chimney! It's time to re-mortgage, because by the sound of it, these guys intend to be here for the long run, to squeeze every penny they can out of your house lid.

Except that almost as soon as they've started, they've suddenly finished. You've paid for a mountain of work, which is, strangely, finished by a single oppo in a morning, with a minimum of materials. The roof is so high, and so hard to monitor casually, that the work that takes place can be anything at all. A big part of this may be 'buttering up', a roofer's term which means that instead of taking off roof parts like ridge tiles and removing their mortar, they simply have mortar raked out and fresh mortar jammed back into the crevice. This is not the way you'd make a Victoria Sandwich cake, and certainly not how to treat the crowning glory of your home. Repairs like these provide a temporary fix at best.

Similarly, soffit and fascia boards are ripe for abuse. Rogues will inevitably find them lacking or rotting, and offer to replace and protect them with white UPVC sheeting. In practice, the wooden boards are not replaced but hidden behind the plastic, which, poorly fitted, traps rain and other moisture inside and guarantees their disintegration, concealed from sight. It's almost tragic.

Flat roofs fare no better. A leaky flat roof should have the wooden boards replaced and new asphalt (now sometimes fibreglass sheeting) applied. But once again there are shortcuts, meaning you'll have a big black sticking plaster over your roof which, most likely, won't get you through the winter. Insist on new boards being fitted, and if you don't see timber, you're not getting the job you paid for.

Roofing really can be a bit Wild-Westy. Personal recommendations are worth a lot, as is a local address you can identify. OOTBNFY is not advice here, it's a holy writ. If someone likes the look of your roof, by definition, it means that they themselves must be pretty roofless.

> This is not the way you'd make a Victoria Sandwich cake, and certainly not how to treat the crowning glory of your home.

LAYING DOWN THE LAW

There's big money at stake with some of these jobs around the house. If you're considering getting someone in to sort out what ails you, then here are a few basics I've developed from my time on Rogue Traders. Nothing is foolproof or copper-bottomed, but these will cut down your chances of getting stuffed.

→ Use the rule of 3x3x3: get three prices from three contractors and plan on at least a three-week wait. Those three weeks take the pressure off the decision and let you prepare for them coming. Any contractor worth their salt usually has at least the next three weeks' work sorted anyway. Don't bother with anyone who gives you a price over the phone.

← My advice used to be to only deal with people who have a landline number, but I've just checked online and now, for just £1.99 a month, I can get a virtual number with an Aberdeen dialing code which comes straight through to my mobile wherever I am, so that advice is now pants. A verifiable bricks-and-mortar address is still worth something, though.

→ Your contractors can come from a number of sources – recommendations from friends, local authority trusted trader lists – but try to source them from somewhere where a bad job means they lose something: local reputation, a licence, membership of a trade body. It's a lovely, liberating feeling to trust someone you've never met to do a good job, like you're welcoming in a new family member. But the harsh truth is we're not making friends here, we're laying block paving. We can all be friends when the job's perfect and everyone's been paid.

← Make sure that they give you a written quote, not an estimate. They are quite different things. Legally, you can hang your hat on a quote. It's legally binding, hard and unshakeable like a bronze statue. An estimate, on the other hand, is one of those wobbly inflatable men you sometimes see advertising garages. You can't hang your hat on it, but you might lose your shirt.

→ In your quote, you want detail for each bit of the job, including materials and labour. That way, if anything changes, as it inevitably will, you can add and subtract based on what you've already got, rather than go into the 'Land of Make Believe', a terrible song by Bucks Fizz.*

---

* The 1982 hit 'The Land of Make Believe' by Bucks Fizz was in fact written by Andy Hill, who also worked with prog rock group King Crimson. Despite its saccharine sweetness, he has revealed that it was written as a protest song against Margaret Thatcher. FACT! You certainly wouldn't have got that from the lyric 'not for all the tea in China'.

← Try to get a start and finish date, and working hours throughout the day. The finish date is always going to have to have a degree of flexibility, as bigger jobs tend to change as they develop. There shouldn't be any flexibility on the start date. These set the expectation and give everyone something to aim for.

→ Make sure you stage the payments across the job, holding back at least 50 per cent until the work is completed. It's got to be written down, as part of the contract. Don't be swayed by protestations that materials need to be bought. Dodgepots often use this excuse as a prelude to walking out on a job after a couple of weeks with 80 per cent of the money in their pockets.

← Pay everyone on time. Everyone needs to get paid. Don't be a rogue customer. Every big job carries a big financial risk for smaller firms. It may be your conservatory, but it's their livelihood.

TRADE BODIES

Pretty much any advice I've read about rogue traders somewhere contains the blanket advice to make sure whoever you hire is accredited by a trade body, federation or association of some kind. I'm not going to do that, because I know that trade bodies are like lasagne: the difference between a good one and a bad one is immense.

Sadly, many exist as dodgy businesses in their own right – a way to make money through fees from the traders who sign up to them – and as a result, they are more likely to take the side of their customers than their customer's customer. It's really hard to expel a member of your association when they've been paying a couple of hundred quid a year to use your logo. Some are even set up by dodgy traders to give them an air of credibility. Membership? One. They offer false trust and are part of the problem, posing as the solution.

Having said that, a few trade associations are genuinely useful, and an even smaller few can be invaluable when choosing a trader. So how do you sort the screwdrivers from the spanners? Here are some questions you should be asking:

→ Does the body have government backing? A few examples, like Gas Safe and NICEIC, do, backed up by legislation that means failure to comply is a legal offence. These bodies may be commercial enterprises, but if they aren't up to muster, the government will choose someone else to do the job. From your point of view, you've got the law on your side

← Does this federation/association have anything to lose if they let me down? Many are granted a Royal Charter by the sovereign, advised by the privy council, which means they have a nationwide approval as the go-to body in their subject. Examples include the Chartered Institute of Architectural Technologists (CIAT) and the Chartered Institute of Housing (CIH). Royal Charters are hard-won and fiercely protected. If your trader is showing membership, make sure it checks out by calling the body direct, and make them your first call (after the trader) if things go wrong.

→ How many members has this body expelled in the last five years? If the answer is 'none' then chances are you're not looking at a body that's useful to you, you're looking at a traders' publicity club that's looking after its members, not customers.

← How seriously do these people take misuse/abuse of their brand/logo? If the badge is worth anything, it should be fiercely protected to make sure that no-one's ripping it off. Search for evidence they've prosecuted offenders before.

→ How easy is it to cross-check membership? A decent association will let you, the person who's about to spend thousands of pounds based on the trust they're giving, check out membership numbers against names and photos. This means that the guy in your airing cupboard is who he says he is, and that you've got a comeback if he floods your lounge through the ceiling. Without this ability, your association is virtually useless, as a single ID card could be used by 20 operatives, and yet you wouldn't believe how few associations do it.

.chapter
nine

Cars

Believe the ads and it's living the dream: just slide your bum across the driver's seat, grab the wheel and you're in control of your destiny. But a new car is also one of the biggest buys you'll ever make, and the road to happy motoring can be cratered with potholes which can eat up your cash and leave you walking to work past a metal mickey-taker on your drive. However you buy your car, there are ways to win and lose, so switch to cruise and check out our car-buyer's roadmap. It'll keep you on the road and out of trouble.

What you gain on the swings you can lose on the roundabouts, particularly if it's one of the thousands of roundabouts in Milton Keynes.

BUYING A SECOND-HAND CAR

I like buying things second hand, particularly when it comes to a motor. It means that if there's anything fundamentally wrong with the thing, it should have gone wrong for the first owner. Add to that the fact that new cars lose at least a quarter of their value in the first year of ownership, and you've got a compelling reason to take a car that's been pre-loved. But as with anything, what you gain on the swings you can lose on the roundabouts, particularly if it's one of the thousands of roundabouts in Milton Keynes. Buying a second-hand car still means you save, but there can be bumps in the road, particularly if you come up against someone who's determined to hide the true history of your prospective motor. And I've met a few of them.

Technology is your friend

If you want to buy a second-hand car, there's now plenty you can do without leaving your chair. Start by working out a budget, not just for the car itself but for all the extras including fuel, insurance, road tax, tyres, the lot. No point having a Merc that's too dear to get you to work. Better to have a Ford you can afford.

Cars with smaller engines tend to be cheaper to run and make great run-arounds, but if you are hauling long distances across the country something with a bigger engine and a greater degree of comfort may be a better option.

Then consider what's going in the tank, and how it affects your bank. Diesel cars have bigger price tags and are currently a bit more expensive to fill at the pumps, but they tend to be more durable and have better economy than petrol. The real question is what governments feel about diesels. After years of telling us they were the way forward, they've changed their minds, convinced by evidence that clearly shows the nitrous oxide they pump out is harming us all more than we'd realised. Modern diesels, conforming to the latest guidelines, are better, but still not great, even compared to buses and trucks, which are more strictly regulated. If you are going to buy a diesel car (and there are 13 million out there on the road, so you wouldn't be a total pariah) then make sure you know which Euro-standard it complies with. This could make a difference when you come to entering low-emission zones in cities here and abroad.

Petrol is the safe choice for now – although that will change, as sales will be banned by 2035. The braver choice is, of course, electric or hybrid, but you will end up paying more up-front for these models, then typically saving in the long run on refuelling and running costs like the rock-bottom road tax. Electric cars also tend to hold their value much better than their petrol or diesel alternatives, which, by the way, are round the back of the bike sheds, having a fag.

Do you prefer manual gearboxes or automatics, which are probably more expensive to purchase but may be less costly to run? If you've got kids in their teens, and the patience of a saint, it's worth having a manual motor for

> *Are you still in that chair? OK, stand up and do some stretches, then sit back down again.*

them to learn in. Lots of families these days go for an SUV, because they look smart and you can, according to the adverts, park them on clifftops to look at the sea. OK, if that's what you want, but you'll often get less boot space, poorer fuel economy and less room inside than the estate car your parents drove.

Are you still in that chair? OK, stand up and do some stretches, then sit back down again. Before you leave the house and risk catching a chill, read as many online reviews as possible for your shortlist of motors. Most will give an idea of common problems and shortcomings, but be warned, most drivers like to convince themselves and others that they've bought the best car on earth. You tend to get five- or one-star reviews and not much in between. Check out auto mags for a more objective comparison.

Where to buy

Right. I think we may be ready to put on a coat and stout footwear and actually go outside to see a car. And when you finally do, you've got a range of options, typically: dealerships, private sales, auctions and online platforms.

DEALERSHIPS

You'll pay more from a main dealer. What you should get is peace of mind. Look for an established firm with a solid reputation. Part of that peace of mind should be a warranty: an agreement that they'll at least fix things if they go wrong within a given period. Don't accept at face value that this is what the warranty does, though. They are often financial arrangements with a third-party group, a bit like insurance. I've heard from too many people who have been fobbed off by garages when they've gone to claim on a warranty. Inspect it like you would the car. Some warranties are jam-packed with exclusions that can leave you paying for expensive repairs soon after purchase, so take time to check it. If in doubt, put money aside monthly for car repairs rather than committing to a leaky scheme. Usually the best warranties are the ones issued by the manufacturer at the point of sale. If your car is nearly new (under five years) there's a chance that this will still have some time to run.

> *Some warranties are jam-packed with exclusions that can leave you paying for expensive repairs soon after purchase, so take time to check it.*

It's worth checking the calendar before you go car shopping. Car salespeople have quarterly sales targets to meet at the end of March, June, September and December. Make an offer in the weeks leading up to these deadlines and you could get a better deal than otherwise.

Now, we've identified a car we like. It matches our requirements. What do we do? We do NOT tell the salesperson. Instead, we ask about a price, staying polite but detached. The salesperson is not our new friend. We will, if everything goes right, never see them after today.

Crucially, repeat after me:

> *I'm a haggler.*

> *I like to haggle.*

> *I was born to haggle, and I will fight for the best price.*

> *I am, in fact Marvin Haggler.*

And this is the order of haggling:

> *Price – Warranty – Extras – Finance*

Your price is the headline. It's your starting point, not your end destination, so make sure you get it out nice and early. After that, your haggling technique is simply raising a series of reasons why the car is just not right, however perfect it may be. You and I know that this is the only Saturday you have free for the next four months, and that you desperately need this car otherwise your daughter's cello lessons won't happen. The salesperson must never, ever know this. They don't get their commission without your permission. Squeeze the lowest price you can, then go in again for a longer warranty. When that's tapped out, go around the car again, looking for anything that drives the value down. Mileage, colour, wheel trim, seat colour, engine size, fuel type, economy, whatever you can find. And don't forget, silence is golden. It invites friendly salespeople to fill it by offering something new. Having somewhere else to be and walking away are always good for a couple of reasons. You get time to think without Smiling Jim breathing down your neck, and it makes him have a long, hard think about how much he wants your custom. Finally, when you've got the best deal you can, ask him this question:

'And what would the cash price be?'

Yes, you're saying that you can buy the car outright, without finance. POW! Marvin Haggler!

It should be cheaper because the finance company isn't getting its cut. But not always. Often dealers make money from the finance deal, so they'll prefer you to take it. At the very least you stand the chance of seeing a difference in price, possibly a cut.

However strong you feel your position is, unless your daughter is actually outside, shivering, with her cello (poor parenting), don't sign on the day. Take away a written quote with everything outlined and check the prices of any other items thrown in with the car package, in case those hidden costs have inexplicably risen. You might live close to a car supermarket which has new and nearly new cars but remember, this isn't the same as a regular dealer. It's likely to have numerous competitively priced cars from a range of manufacturers under one roof but almost certainly won't offer the same after-sales service.

Don't forget, silence is golden.

Matt Nav

In 2018, there were 39.4 million registered vehicles on the roads of the United Kingdom – a number that's increased virtually every year since the Second World War – with an average age of 8.2 years.

I've come across some proper dodgy car dealers in the past and it's fair to say they couldn't have sold cars if they hadn't been friendly and charming, at least to start with. But what a difference a day (and a cashed cheque) makes! In one case, we returned a car which was not just a lemon, it was a whole bag of citrus fruit. The boss, who we hadn't dealt with before, told us we would get our money back 'when he died' and then pushed us out the gates. As we went, he squirted bottles, and then threw a bucket of water over us. We went back a couple of days later, and the car lot was empty, and the buildings had been torched.

Mate! We only wanted a refund! Talk about an overreaction!

PRIVATE SALES

Rule number one: never, EVER buy a car you've seen with a mobile number on a piece of paper by the side of the road. That way heartache lies. This is the way that unofficial dealers offload their death-trap junksters, and they do so because there is absolutely no comeback if (when) things go wrong with it. There are laws to prevent selling cars this way, but they don't work, and no-one's really enforcing them. The nastiest rogue I ever came across was selling cars this way. He offered to sort me out good and proper after the show, and I'd rather you didn't meet him. I'm sorry to have to speak sternly about this matter, but it's because I care for you.

Privately sold cars are higher risk, higher reward. They could be a bargain but won't have undergone the same health checks, so there's lots more to watch out for when it comes to doorstep transactions. Your rights are the same in theory – protection by the Consumer Rights Act of 2015 (see p. 10) – but in practice they work quite differently. The owner of the car doesn't have to tell you about any faults with the car, because they genuinely can't be expected to know about them. You would have to demonstrate that you'd been misled to stand a chance of winning your case. In practice, this would mean obtaining a piece of paper which stated 'I can state that this car is in perfect working order' before purchase. Not gonna happen. So it's more of a roll of the dice, but there are things you can do to armour-plate your deal:

➡ If the car is advertised as 'sold as seen' then move on.

⬅ Go to the seller's home and check the address matches that on the log book. They won't want you coming back if the car goes kerplunk. It's just a little bit of insurance.

➡ Ask why the car is being sold and keep a copy of the original small ad for reference. Any details that later prove not to be true could be the basis of legal action.

⬅ Mileage is a moveable feast these days. If it says 20,000 on the clock, but the rubber on the pedals has gone through and you can tell what jeans the owner wears by looking at the driver's seat, someone's been tinkering.

➡ Fridge magnets! Closely inspect the car in daylight and good weather. Changes in the texture of the paintwork and a magnet that won't stick mean your car may have been in a shunt or might be a cut-and-shut: the wrong kind of hybrid, two written-off cars joined together to make a Frankencar. Experts reckon there are 30,000 possibly lethal cut-and-shuts on the roads in the UK. Check for uneven panels and examine the top of the rear windscreen carefully, as this is a common join.

← Look at the corner of the windscreen where the Vehicle Identification Number (VIN) and registration number are engraved. Any hint of tampering or a mismatch, and this car is for someone else, my friend.

→ Open and shut all the doors, the boot and the bonnet. Flick all the switches and levers. If they feel wrong, something's happened to this car that it didn't like. Press a 20p coin into a tyre channel. If the tread hides the outer rim of the coin, it's legal. Press down on each corner of the car, to test suspension. If it rises back into its original position, that's a good sign.

← Peek beneath the car to make sure nothing is leaking.

→ Even if you're a novice, put your head under the bonnet and check the oil, using the dipstick. Muddy oil means poor maintenance. If the inside of the oil cap has a thick, white substance clinging to it, that could be a sign of engine damage. The coolant should be bright blue. If it's rust coloured, the engine may well have been running without anti-freeze, and you could be the one catching a cold later on. Take a snap of the engine number while you're there, to check later against the one listed in the log book.

As long as they're not critical flaws, you can use any of the things you spot during this inspection as a haggling tool, to bargain down the price at the end of the process.

Matt Nav

Technology is not your friend. Bizarrely, it's never been easier to muck about with the mileage of a car. Remember that scene from *Ferris Bueller's Day Off* where they try to run back the clock by jacking up the axle and letting it run in reverse? Well, it used to be that or some jiggery-pokery with an electric drill. Great news, dodgepots! Faking mileage and inflating value now just means downloading software, plugging your laptop into the diagnostic port of a car, and typing in the new mileage. I've seen it done! Crazy, exciting times we live in.

It's not actually a crime to tinker with the mileage of a car, but it is a crime to sell it on with a faked mileage, as I pointed out to the leader of a gang in the Midlands who was doing just that, subtracting enough miles from various cars to go halfway to the moon. We tested this by selling him a car, and then buying it back with – magically – half the mileage on it. To make up for this subtraction he added a few miles by running away down the A38 to get away from us.

AUCTIONS

If you have the heart of a lion and the mechanical knowledge of Enzo Ferrari, why not try buying a car at an auction? Seriously, there may be bargains there, but you'll be surrounded by people who are there week in, week out who really know what they're doing. Yes, there are no doubt terrific bargains on the conveyor belt of vehicles on display but you'll get a few minutes for a cursory inspection at best before you're launched into a feverish bidding process. As you can imagine, it's not an environment that allows for a considered approach to buying the thing you're going to strap your family into before hurtling down the M6. I'm not saying don't do it. I'm just saying I wouldn't do it. But then I've never presented *Top Gear*.

ONLINE PLATFORMS

Similarly fun/disastrous can be buying a car unseen on the internet. There are many apparently easy options these days which seem to take the slog out of buying a car, delivering it hundreds of miles to your door and even taking your old car as part exchange. The reality is that car dealers don't operate as charities. They won't risk delivery costs and accepting your car unseen unless there's something in it for them. Usually this means overpricing the car you're going to get. It might seem like a bargain or convenient, but you won't be saying that at 5.30 on a cold and frosty morning when your engine warning light shouts, 'I told you so!'

Test driving isn't just for Lewis Hamilton

You're probably getting the feeling that the time you take getting to know a car before you part with any money is time well spent. I wouldn't disagree at all. Sitting behind the wheel for the first time, ask yourself some simple questions. Can I reach everything? Can I see everything I need to see? Listen to the way the car starts and the noises it makes when the engine turns over, and look for lights that come on and stay on. A test drive should last at least 30 minutes so that you can try out different road surfaces and speeds. Check the temperature gauge. If the vehicle has been warmed up already, you need to ask why, as it should start first time when the engine is stone cold. Blue-black smoke billowing from the exhaust is a danger sign.

> A test drive should last at least 30 minutes so that you can try out different road surfaces and speeds.

Traffic is good to see how the car takes off and brakes.

Traffic is good to see how the car takes off and brakes. If it struggles to go, there could be a problem with the clutch – expensive. If the brakes feel uneven or weak or make a noise, don't go any further without an inspection. The clutch and gears should feel smooth, not stiff or sloppy, and listen carefully (radio off!) for any bumping and grinding in the engine or the suspension. Check the radio (radio on!). The steering wheel should feel light under your hands, but not too light, in which case it may have just fallen off. A definite no-no.

Head to a flat, deserted road and take your hands off the wheel for a moment at a slow speed, to see if the vehicle tracks either left or right. At the same safe spot, try braking suddenly to gauge the vehicle's response. Go to a hilly area to put the handbrake through its paces. If you buy, don't forget to get car tax as it's no longer transferable.

Matt Nav

If you went into a dealer for a test drive, you'd think that you'd be automatically insured, wouldn't you? Of course you would! But while making the programme we've often been allowed to test drive cars that should never have been on the road, and if we hadn't had our own insurance we wouldn't have been covered.

Non-dodgy dealers will have special insurance to cover test drives but it probably won't be the case with private sales. Check your own insurance, which may well permit you to drive another car with the owner's permission, and take the paperwork with you if it does. There is always an awkward moment in a private sale where the buyer wants to test drive, but the seller doesn't want to hand over the keys. The best solution is for buyer and seller to go together. This doesn't work so well on motorbikes, unless they're really good friends. The solution is often for the buyer to hand over the full cash price before taking her for a spin. The whole thing is, frankly, awks.

What to look out for

Little things mean a lot. Check there is a second key, a spare tyre where applicable, a functional jack kit and a manual. Also look out for a servicing booklet and, where applicable, a sales contract and details of the finance package. And of course it should come with a log book, or V5C as it's officially called. The log book – check for the watermark that runs through its front facing page – shows who the car is registered to, not necessarily who owns it. Instantly it reveals the VIN and also the engine number so you can compare those with the vehicle.

Even with all of this, not many of us could spot if there were something seriously wrong with a car. Luckily there are a load of people now who can poke and probe on our behalf. The big motoring organisations offer a checking service, which might cost a hundred quid or more, but which is still cheaper than a clunky clutch.

OK! Done all that? Right, now it's time to come in off the forecourt, back to our cosy nook, and stick the kettle on again because… technology is our friend!

→ Check the car's MOT history online at the DVLA website. MOTs also give you a history of mileage, which should run in a nice, steady line to the current figure. If not, ask yourself why. And if the last recorded MOT mileage is higher than what's on the clock, run away from the car and call the police. You can also check if the car is taxed or on a SORN (untaxed but hasn't been on the road).

← Use the Money Advice Service car costs calculator to find out estimated running costs. Make sure it's affordable.

→ Do an online data check. There are scores of sites that offer this and it will reveal if the car has been stolen or is an insurance write-off, or if there's outstanding finance. If there is, the car could be re-possessed even with a change in registration documents. Many cars are legally sold on as insurance write-offs, but you must be told.

If you've done all these checks and you decide to buy, make sure you get a written receipt showing the make, model and VIN of the car, the identity and address of the vendor, your own address and the amount paid. In addition, get whatever assurances they are willing to offer about the quality of the car. Anything they've said to you in person, they should be willing to commit to writing. It should be signed by both sides, and sealed with a kiss. OK. Maybe that's going too far.

Matt Nav

Vehicle checkers HPI say one in three cars has a hidden past, one in five has had a number plate change, and one in 14 has mileage discrepancies. That's a lot of dodgepots selling cars. We know from making the programme that a good way to scale up flogging clunkers is to make your huge dodgy used-car business look like a series of private sales. The rules are different, much easier to get around, and it's harder to track down a private seller when things go wrong. What's making it even harder is that the old advice – always go with someone who uses a landline over a mobile phone – doesn't work any more. The phone industry has now deregulated land lines so they aren't geographically locked. What looks like a bricks-and-mortar landline can be simply a floating number that's assigned to a mobile.

Thanks, phone industry guys. Thanks a lot!

BUYING A
NEW CAR

Hmmmm. That smell. That's it, isn't it? Being the first bum on the driver's seat of a new car is, apparently, something special. No tissues in the side pockets and no little foot marks on the back of the seats. But new cars still go wrong, and people who sell new cars can be as honest as the day is long. A day in February. In Northern Finland.

OK, so the process starts the same way: armchair research time until you've got your shortlist based on fuel, transmission, your personal needs, etc. But that's when you need to change tack. You're buying new, you crazy thing, so you can check what's going on with the manufacturer. There may be slight fluctuations and room for Marvin Haggling, but the manufacturer's website will give you a pretty clear idea of where you can start with negotiations, along with current offers, special editions and the rest of it.

A quick word about special editions: they can be great, with heated seats and radios that you wouldn't have got earlier in the model's lifetime, but they are a bit like your single, sixty-year-old uncle Alf buying a new hat in the hope of getting lucky at a family wedding. They are a sign that a new model or an upgrade is fast approaching, and that loveable though the old model is, its value should be put in that context. Sorry Alf, the truth hurts. Nice hat.

So you know your requirements, and you're ready to visit the dealership. The same rules of Marvellous Marvin Haggling apply. Stay happy and non-committal. Play your cards close to your chest, and your credit cards closer still. Even if you know exactly what you want, you are a person with options, and crucially, the money is still in your account. The time you spend with the salesperson is special. This purchase will be important for you both. You appreciate his skill and approachability. You are grateful for the free coffee he served you after pressing a button. This does not make you friends.

No car is perfect. A new car even less so, because as soon as you drive it off the forecourt you're effectively chucking money out the window. Just like on a movie set, beware of extras that don't appear to be doing anything useful. If they're part of the stated price, find out their value, and get them stripped out to get the price down. If you didn't think you needed them on the way in, you certainly don't want to be paying hundreds for them. Test drive, but know it's not the car you'll be getting. It could be bells and whistles to impress or Billy Basic to keep costs down.

> *Stay happy and non-committal. Play your cards close to your chest, and your credit cards closer still.*

> *Warning! Sales should be made from reputable dealers and definitely not from a dealer's registered stock.*

Again, as long as the money is in your pocket, you're in control of the time frame. The usual salesperson way to counter this easy and enjoyable state of mind is to instil the fear that the deal that's being offered is only available for a limited time. It may be. But cars are rolling off of production lines at an incredible rate. Special offers are binned and reintroduced with a fanfare and frequency only eclipsed by managers of Chelsea Football Club. 2.5 million new cars are sold every year. There will be another one along in a minute, so don't sweat it. Take your time.

There's certainly time to check out a car broker. Accessible through the internet, it's their job to hunt down the best deal for you. Usually ex-car traders themselves, they can strike cool, bulk-buy deals and, best of all, they shouldn't seek up-front payment. (If they do, they're not for you.) Brokers will charge the dealership 1 per cent when a sale is made. Warning! Sales should be made from reputable dealers and definitely not from a dealer's registered stock. If that happens, your name won't appear first on the registration document. That ups the numbers of registered owners and brings the value down. What's the upside to brokers? You might get the same car at a good discount, with warranty and the plastic still on the seats. Downside? The broker might source nationwide. You could be travelling to Galashiels to pick it up. That's fine, as long as you live near Galashiels.

FINANCING YOUR CAR

So you need a car. How you gonna pay?

Cash was once king. The immediacy of the queen's head on paper used to turn heads and drop prices. No longer. Finance deals can bring with them a kickback for the dealer over time. It's the gift that keeps giving, with sales targets all of its own, so you can find your salesperson disappointed that you're flashing the cash. Still a potent weapon for private sales though – in fact, often the only thing some sellers will take to avoid being stiffed.

Nowadays, many of us will need some kind of credit arrangement in place. So here's the tricky bit. Money. The moment of sitting in your new car lasts exactly that. A moment. But unless you are a premiership footballer or hedge-fund manager, chances are that the payments will last long after the thrill has gone and the kids have spilled apple juice down the upholstery. Your crucial term here is Annual Percentage Rate (APR). It should be an apples-with-apples point of comparison for borrowing, or for that matter, saving. Many car dealers advertise an APR for their finance, but the reality is a bit more complex. They only have to give that APR to 51 per cent of customers – dependent on their circumstances – to be able to stick it up in lights. The problem is that you won't know if you're in the lucky 51 per cent or the other 49 per cent until you apply, and a rejection means your credit score could be affected, right?

Well, yes and no. You can have a dummy run at applying for credit. It's called a 'soft' or 'smart' search, which means you can ask the question without your name being attached. A bit like being twelve, fancying someone but saying that it's your friend who's interested. A bit like that.

You have a few options when it comes to finance:

Personal loan

This means borrowing a lump sum over a set term, usually from a bank. The car's yours, whatevs; the money sitch is between you and the bank.

Hire purchase

After you make (usually) a 10 per cent deposit, the finance company operating this arrangement owns the car until the last payment is made. Fail to keep up the payments and your car could be leaving you with little or no notice. Some cars sold on hire purchase even have tracking devices to make repossession easier. Feels a bit KGB, doesn't it?

Personal contract purchase

Hire purchase without the purchase bit. You pay a deposit and monthly payments for a set time, but these cover only the depreciation of the car, not its full value, so it's cheaper. There may be a mileage cap. If you want to keep the vehicle at the end of the agreement, there's the opportunity to hand over what's called a 'balloon payment' to cover the market cost of the car. Alternatively, give back the vehicle and start all over again with a new one!

Personal contract hire

More like a lease, this runs for a fixed period. It can include, at extra cost, a maintenance agreement. Like a PCP, there might be a mileage cap – make sure it's right for you. You never actually own the vehicle, but then you don't worry about it losing value either. The kicker often comes if you want to terminate the agreement, or if you go over the agreed mileage, or fail to keep the car in good nick. You will need a fully comprehensive insurance policy.

Credit card

Obviously, if you're using the card to cover the whole purchase, your borrowing limit will dictate what you can buy, but there are upsides to using it for a deposit as you get some cover from Section 75 of the Consumer Credit

Act (see p. 23) if things all go a bit Kim Il Jong. The massive downside is that APR on credit cards is Himalayan, so best not leave that debt there for longer than you absolutely have to. Credit cards are also excellent for removing ice from the windscreen on cold mornings.

Matt Nav

People between the ages of 25 and 44 borrow on average £9,633 to buy a car, according to Moneysupermarket. com, with January the most popular month to take out a loan. Again, affordability is the key. Missing your rent because you've not done your sums on a car loan means you're putting everything at risk. You won't like your car so much if you have to sleep in it. One rule of thumb is that you shouldn't spend more than 35 per cent of your annual income on your car – that's everything, including finance, fuel, insurance and road tax. You should try to spend much less if you can, but certainly no more. If you're struggling to find good finance, don't be tempted by dealers who offer easy options. I've seen so many customers end up being sold cars they desperately need on finance, only for those cars to let them down within weeks. You're better off saving for longer to put down a bigger deposit with a reliable dealer than spending years paying for a car you can't use.

INSURANCE

Insurance isn't optional, but Jiminy Cricket can it be expensive. Driving uninsured risks a hefty fine, points on your licence and your vehicle being impounded and possibly crushed to the size of a pea. But it's taken seriously for a reason. Those who drive without insurance are costing the country £256 million per year, according to the Motor Insurance Bureau, which works out to an extra £15 per premium. But like anything, there's a good way and a bad way to get insured. We are here to ensure you pick the former.

Buying insurance

Who you are and what you've done make a big difference when you're getting insured. Your age, experience, vehicle, job and where you live are all important, but insurers place different emphasis on each of those, so shopping around and comparing really is important, as is looking in detail at what's being offered. The level of cover can also vary massively from one company to another, as can customer service. It's tempting, especially for newer drivers who insurers charge like a cavalry division, to make your decision based on who has the lowest price, but when you come to claim, those little differences can make a big difference.

THE BASICS

Insurance cover comes in three flavours:

Third party: this is the minimum level of cover you can take out, and legally you have to have it. At least if you cause an accident, any damage to the other person's car or property will be covered. Your car won't be though, so you'll have to pay to get it fixed. If someone else causes the accident, their insurance should cover you… as long as they have it.

→ Third party, fire and theft: all of the above, but your policy will also pay out if your car is stolen or damaged by fire.

← Fully comprehensive: this is the only product that will compensate you if you are in an accident. Always check fully comp rates as the margin between these three types can be pretty small, when you take into account what you get.

Cars come with an insurance group, a number from 1–50 which can make a big difference to your premium. Group 1 tend to be less powerful cars which are safer, cheap and easy to repair, so they're cheaper to insure. A group 50 car, on the other hand, tends to be powerful, expensive to fix, and driven by someone who thinks a lot of themselves.

NO CLAIM, ALL GAIN

Counting against the potentially mammoth cost of insurance is the magical No Claims Bonus. This is a reward for not hitting things, which, over the years, can result in huge discounts to your premium. Another way of keeping the cost of premiums down is to juggle with the amount of excess you're prepared to pay. This means that in the event of an accident, you will take a hit for the first, say £200, and your insurers only pay over and above that. Double that excess to £400, and the insurer shakes you warmly by the hand and lowers your premium. A bit. Some other ideas to help you save:

➤ Never lie to an insurance company. However, there are often different, equally accurate ways of describing your job on their forms, which can result in a reduced premium.

← If you move house, you can save. East London is the most expensive area to insure in, while the Isle of Man is the cheapest. I wouldn't make that the only reason for moving there, but there it is.

➤ Insurers often stick on extras that you don't need which nudge up the price. You may already have windscreen replacement or a European breakdown service. Some offer a courtesy car if yours is off the road. Do you want it? If not, don't pay for it.

- Some insurers charge an administration fee for claims. You might not know about it until an accident happens.

- Don't auto-renew. Like Christmas, the chance to get cheaper insurance only comes once a year, so let's celebrate it. Like other bills, you WILL save money.

INSURING YOUNG PEOPLE

How weird is this? With the exception of the Trump kids, young people don't have much money, and yet they pay on average around three times as much for their insurance as their parents. Or at least, when their parents aren't paying for it as well (grumble curse grumble).

Less experience behind the wheel means, statistically, younger drivers are more likely to have an accident. But there are steps to take that will hopefully bring your insurance in line with the average amount, just a shade under a four-figure sum:

- Group 1. Group 1. Group 1. The answer is a Vauxhall Corsa. Or a Fiat Panda. Others are, of course, available.

- Passed your test? Now pass another. Some companies offer a price reduction for a Pass Plus. Money up front, but safer driving and lower premiums.

- Consider getting a black box installed to monitor speed and braking, which helps companies reward good driving (see box opposite).

- Add a named driver with a good driving record as a secondary user (although remember the main driver is the one who uses the vehicle most).

- If possible, pay up front as monthly instalments may be more expensive.

- Offer to pay a bigger excess – although be aware this will substantially reduce the amount you will receive in the aftermath of any collision.

Matt Nav

Black boxes are a miracle – a way to sort the sheep from the goats, if what you mean by goats is reckless younger drivers. The boxes came in a few years back and promised to bring premiums down for younger drivers by monitoring how you drive, rather than making lazy assumptions based on age and experience. I've met a lot of very good newly qualified drivers. And some terrible ones. The problem is that on *Watchdog* we've seen the black box technology isn't always totally reliable. One driver had her insurance cancelled after she was recorded by her black box doing 119 mph in her Skoda Fabia. Now, to be fair to the insurers, this is possible in theory, if the Skoda Fabia in question is going downhill, has the wind behind it, and is fitted with some kind of rocket propulsion system.

REPAIRING YOUR CAR

Dodgy garages. Sigh.

You have to trust them because, frankly, if you knew anything about cars you would have fixed the thing yourself. But once they are alone with your car, who knows what they're doing, right?

Luckily, most garages are honest and swift to help. A few aren't. Steel yourself, and carry these words of wisdom into battle:

→ Be clear and detailed when you outline the problem with the car. Find out as much as you can before going in, particularly in relation to the cost of any parts that may be needed.

← Insist that any unexpected work is only carried out after permission is given, and that all costs must be itemised. Any parts replaced must be retained and receipts for purchase handed over with the bill. Don't expect to make any friends by asking for this, but it's easier to have five minutes of argy bargy before than six months after.

→ The law says repairs have to be done with 'reasonable skill and care' and you are due a price drop if that didn't happen. But it's a wibbly wobbly phrase, and would need a second opinion at least to make it mean anything in a court.

← The garage can keep your car if the bill is in dispute. If you're unhappy but want your car, consider paying the bill marked 'paying under protest'. It means you haven't surrendered your right to battle on.

→ If the garage is a member of a trade body that claims to protect the consumer, get them on board as soon as possible. Some of these bodies are useless, for-profit businesses (see p. 287), and some aren't. But every bit of pressure helps, and it's cheaper than going to court.

← If you remain convinced the garage is acting unlawfully, contact Trading Standards.

chapter
ten

Travel

What's better, and slightly more expensive, than staying at home? Travel! If nothing else, getting out to see the world makes you truly realise just how much you enjoy home. Seriously, holidays are great, but they're a big chunk of money just waiting to fall into the wrong hands for a duff deal. Let's send that idea packing!

Matt Stat

Since 2018, Package Travel has had its own set of laws – the Package Travel Regulations (PTRs) and its kinda wimpy little brother, the Linked Travel Arrangements. In essence, if you book more than one element – flight, accommodation or car hire – at the same time, the provider must compensate you for any changes or, in the case of cancellation, refund you within 14 days. COVID-19 has put these to the test like never before, with many companies simply failing to refund. As I write, it's playing out and we don't know how government, the industry and consumer groups will resolve this. But the PTRs are your rights in law – and whatever you're told, they can't be taken away or superseded by company policy.

PACKAGE HOLIDAYS

For most of us, this is what holidays have looked like since the middle of the 19th century, when Thomas Cook (don't, it's still raw) ran a church social trip by train from Leicester to the sun-kissed beaches and spicy souks of exotic Loughborough, a whole 11.6 miles away. This was the prototype of the modern all-inclusive, except that your wristband would have got you as much orange squash as you liked, because Thomas Cook was a fierce teetotaller.

The tone for package holidays was really set after the Second World War though, when firms like Horizon could negotiate great deals and bring overseas travel to people who wouldn't have dreamt of it previously. This period also gave rise to every bad joke you've ever heard about package holidays: chips-with-everything greasy food, delays, concrete hotels reminiscent of Stalinist detention centres, and excursions that gave the general feeling that you were on the wrong end of the scale between human and livestock.

I've covered loads of stories on package travel, particularly when I started out on *Watchdog* in the late 90s. Back then there would be a representative of one of the big companies in studio almost every week to account for poor quality accommodation or disrupted travel plans. I'm sure it resulted in a better, slicker travel industry, which has enjoyed a bit of a comeback in recent years… until COVID-19.

The travel ban has shredded people's travel plans and created a money vacuum for the industry. Customers insisted on their rights under the PTR 2018 to get refunds, while companies maintained that to do so would see them go under. They offered vouchers and credit notes instead, but without the protection of ATOL (see below), which the holidays themselves carried. What a mess.

> If you hold your nerve, you can often swoop in on a deal.

Many customers who were tolerant of the disruption lost their patience with thousands of their pounds still sitting in company bank accounts, effectively bankrolling them through the crisis.

Looking for a positive? Well, it does go to highlight how package holidays are protected in ways other travel isn't. And the advantages don't stop there – the providers are also big players, coming back season after season, and that negotiating power means that you'll normally pay less than if you book it yourself. Operators bulk-buy cheaply with airlines and hoteliers months before the summer season, to bring the price down. (Sometimes the cost of an off-the-peg holiday is less than a flight to the same destination.) It's also a really competitive market meaning that if you hold your nerve, you can often swoop in on a deal when there are flash sales as well as last minute reductions. Holidays firms lumbered with pre-bought bed spaces sometimes find they have to off-load them, sharpish, so they don't lose money.

Here's how to unwrap a package holiday bargain:

→ The secret to great comedy is… timing. And the same goes for booking your holiday. Aim to leave on the day after term ends, and you'll be at the peak of peak. Leave it 'til mid-to-late August and you'll see a noticeable drop in prices, and a willingness to do deals. You might even want to see if the family can take a break in the October half-term. You'll get a real bargain, and the queue for the buffet will be much shorter. Lobster, anyone?

← Get in the zone. Again, timing. Anything from eight weeks before departure is squeaky-bum time for travel firms nervous about ending up with empty rooms and flights. Don't sit around in flip flops and sombreros waiting for an on-the-day deal though. By that time, most operators have given up hope.

→ The name's Haggler, Marvin Haggler. Yes, the price you see advertised is your starting point. But it shouldn't be your end point. It can also be an illusion. Headline prices are there to draw the eye, but they sometimes miss out important and unavoidable charges you'll have to pay, slowly but surely pumping up the price like a lilo on a hot day. If you can't deliver a knockout blow on the main price, see if you can jab away at the extras like insurance, excursions and car hire to bring the overall cost down. Go for an upgrade on flights and rooms.

← Be flexible. Most package deals are limited to seven, ten or 14 days. If your dates are ballpark, rather than pinpoint, you'll stand a better chance of Costa Brava without Costa Lotta.

→ If you're not going to leave it late, go early. Early-bird deals can be really attractive, with price drops and free stuff chucked in. You might even be able to pay over time, with just a little deposit.

One great advantage of going with a package tour operator is the presence of resort reps. What a job they do, being on call 24/7 to deal with delays, gripes, illness, bad behaviour, hurricanes and flooding – an almost endless list of scrapes that we might get ourselves into on holiday. I reckon they are among the most positive, capable and tolerant people around, and I salute them.

ATOL protection

ATOL is the Air Travel Organisers' Licensing scheme, first introduced in 1973 by the Civil Aviation Authority, who regulate air travel in the UK and are backed up by the government. A bit like the PTRs it's an undodgeable legal requirement that travel businesses who offer any two or more elements of flight, accommodation or car hire together must be ATOL protected. It does cover some flights – often charter flights, but not usually scheduled flights with an airline, unless specifically stated.

Why is it so amazing? Well, possibly without knowing it, you've been paying £2.50 each and every time you've flown off on holiday. The CAA has been keeping that in a jar on its mantlepiece, called the Air Travel Trust. If your holiday firm or the airline it's using goes bust or is unable to get you home for any reason, they'll get that jar down and use it to get you home. A certificate proving you are ATOL protected is issued when the holiday is booked and it's important to put that in your suitcase, along with your sunscreen and hat, just in case the worst happens.

It distresses me to report that some companies claim to be in ATOL when they are not. Look out for warning signs like:

→ The logo is shown without an identifying number

← Prices are abnormally cheap

Matt Nav

Well, this seems like the right time to come back to the demise of old 'just a tea for me' Tommy Cook. When his business bit the dust in September 2019, it left 155,000 holidaymakers up in the air – some literally (lols)! Not lols, actually. The effort to get them home was gargantuan, the UK's largest peacetime repatriation, eclipsing the collapse of Monarch in 2017. Estimates of the cost of this manoeuvre are over £100 million, most of which will come out of the CAA's Air Travel Trust jar. This has left the jar, which had around £170 million in it before, a bit rattly to say the least. There is a lot of talk that the £2.50 ATOL fee may have to go up if ATOL protection is to work when the next bit of tourist turbulence comes along. Watch this airspace!

According to UK law at the moment, travel businesses based in the UK must subscribe to ATOL.

→ Online enquiry forms don't work

← There's no postal address shown for the company

→ Payment is requested by bank transfer or wire service

← After paying a deposit, you are offered a better deal on the proviso you pay in full

→ The document or email reserving your holiday doesn't bear the logo of the airline concerned. If the company you book with isn't advertising its links to ATOL then ask for its unique four- or five-digit ATOL number that proves it is part of the scheme. Its name should also appear on the ATOL database. According to UK law at the moment, travel businesses based in the UK must subscribe to ATOL.

ABTA Protection: you ABTA have it!

ABTA membership is also worth looking out for. You'll find that 90 per cent of holidays are covered by it. It used to stand for the Association of British Travel Agents, but in practice, it's a trade body that includes a lot of the big tour operators. Again, it's there to provide back up in case your operator fails, in which case you'll either be able to continue your holiday or get your money back. In addition, the ABTA code of conduct provides some guidelines that govern its members. Now you may say, 'Hey, Matt! They're just guidelines!' to which I would answer 'Hey! I know, but

Matt Nav

When Lowcostholidays went into administration in the summer of 2016, 140,000 holidaymakers discovered they had little protection because the company was registered in Spain. Many who were already away had to dip into their holiday funds just to get home. In this deregulated world where it's so easy to register a shell company anywhere you fancy, make sure you don't assume the rules we rely on in the UK are the same ones your travel op is playing by. And, in any case, have good insurance.

failure to abide by a code of conduct constitutes a breach of the 2008 CPFUTR (see p. 16) and that means those guidelines have got legal teeth. Stop shouting! Let's go for a drink sometime!'

Same rules apply with ABTA as with ATOL. Cross-check anyone who uses the badge or name on the ABTA website. They've got a list of members with numbers attached.

Am I packaged or am I linked?

The Linked Travel Regulations give you less protection than the PTRs. You're linked if you've bought the bits within 24 hours from the same platform or agent, but not in the same payment. You'll have protection from the platform in case the first company you bought from – for instance the airline – goes bust – but only while the platform holds the money. It's a lot less useful than the PTRs and a good reason to package everything in one go.

DIY HOLIDAYS

Package holidays aren't for everyone though. Want to leave on a Tuesday for a 23-day trip? Like choosing the time of your flights? Not keen on seeing the same faces on your flight in and out, and at breakfast every morning? Then you'll probably want to go it alone.

You may now see yourself as Indiana Jones, planning your own bespoke travel itinerary, but it's probably going to come at a cost, right? Well, possibly. OK, so you haven't now got the negotiating power of the package holiday companies through bulk buying, but you're also bypassing a legion of middle-people all charging their bit of commission by dealing more directly with airlines, hotels and car hire. That could translate into paying the same, or even less than a convenient package of travel delight. Don't fall into the fool's paradise of ignoring the extra costs of three meals a day though. You're paying for your own trifle now.

Flights

Right! Bullwhip at the ready! Booking flights can be an adventure in itself. You might want to start this journey on a comparison site, but that's not necessarily where the real treasure lies. Many flights won't show up there, and you'll need to do a bit more digging around to find them, going direct to the airlines themselves. But there are traps and pitfalls along the way for the unwary!

For a start, do clicks mean upticks? If you enquire about a price, does it automatically go up a bit the next time you enquire? There's certainly enough anecdotal evidence to suggest that's what happens, with the effect that you're pressured into buying here and now. Instinctively, you think the price is rising because somehow your computer is in cahoots with an airline or holiday company, and together they are driving up costs to push you into an early decision. There are, equally, pretty vehement denials on the part of the airlines that they'd ever do anything of the sort.

> *If you enquire about a price, does it automatically go up a bit the next time you enquire?*

Cookies are to blame, apparently, by which I mean the data that's stored in your web browser about where you've been and what you've clicked. In 2016 a chap over in the US called William McGee decided to test the theory that these cookies can be used to inflate the price of your flight. He and his team carried out 372 flight searches on nine different airline sites, but they did them on two separate computers: one with a history scrubbed of cookies and one with more cookies than a fully-stocked flagship branch of Ben's

Cookies. His results? Wildly inconsistent with either view. Sometimes the scrubbed browser displayed higher prices than the cookieful one. The learning point here, then, is check prices on two different browsers – one clean, one filthy – and then choose the lower of the two, if that's what you get.

Flight platform Skyscanner, which points out that it doesn't make the prices, it just publishes them, says you won't get a cheaper deal by scrubbing your browser. They say fares change by the minute in what's known as a dynamic pricing structure, and as seats are snapped up, so the prices rise. They say the key to getting a deal is flexibility, and staying across changes using email alerts and other tools.

For the computer geeks who are also airline customers, there's the option of changing location on a computer and buying a domestic flight in another country with local currency to take advantage of lower pricing structures there. If you're feeling brave, look in to virtual proxy networks, or, even better, get a (trusted) friend overseas to check the cost, and book it if it's at a worthwhile discount.

Skyscanner shared one valuable tip: having analysed gazillions of bits of data, it can reveal that the best time to book was no later than seven weeks before you want to travel. Another site, Momondo, says the key figure is 53 days rather than 49, and that bookings can then be on average 26 per cent cheaper than booking on departure day. Furthermore, the site advises that Tuesdays, Wednesdays and evenings after 6pm are the cheapest times to fly.

Some carriers offer price guarantees so if you do purchase a ticket and find it cheaper elsewhere you can have the difference refunded. Some companies offer cash, while for others it's in vouchers. These can be used nefariously. We've heard stories of vouchers put up for sale by scam artists who have used stolen credit cards to buy airline tickets, then cancelled them to receive the vouchers, which are subsequently put up for sale at a bargain price. By the time the buyer comes to use the voucher the airline will have discovered the credit card fraud that's taken place and cancelled the voucher. You'll be left with a worthless bit of paper and a lot of suspicious people looking at you.

LAYOVERS AND SPLIT TICKETING

Are you the sort of person who instantly ticks the DIRECT FLIGHT ONLY box when you search for flights? Seriously? When you could have two holidays for the price of one? A few days' break on a long-haul journey not only breaks the monotony but might also save money as the cost of the two legs of the journey can sometimes come in at substantially less than the non-stop equivalent.

Even if you're not planning to leave the airport, you can split up your journey into a series of connecting flights to save money, just like split ticketing with train fares (see p. 369). Great, but miss one and you may miss them all. If they are with the same airline on a single ticket, you'll have more protection if you miss your connection, as the airline may book you onto a later flight. Otherwise, you just become an ordinary person who has come on holiday to Cleveland, Ohio, by mistake. If you've bought a 'through' ticket – with one reservation reference but involving different airlines – it's the airline for the first leg that is responsible for rectifying the issues it has created by being late. Sometimes you can save money by including different and even bizarre legs to a journey, although it takes a level of keyboard confidence to make sure everything fits. Do this and miss a connection and you're Norman No Mates again, ready to discover the delights of Stuttgart Airport until you can afford another ticket.

The cost of the two legs of the journey can sometimes come in at substantially less than the non-stop equivalent.

Matt Nav

Some cities have a number of airports. Make sure that you know which one you're flying into and out of. I had the delight of flying into New York's JFK airport at midnight only to catch a 4am flight from Newark, crossing mid-town New York just as it got kinda crazy. Maybe that's where the band Manhattan Transfer got their name. My son planned his own *Inbetweeners*-style holiday to Malta at 18, good lad. I asked which airport. 'London,' he replied. Er, OK, son. There are five (at least). It turned out to be London Southend. At £24 each way, a cheap flight, OK, but somewhat outweighed by the £160 taxi fare. Other cities are the same, and you can bet budget airlines won't be using the one that's closest, or with the best transport links. The overall winner? Paris-Vatry airport: a staggering 102 miles from the Champs Elysées!

CODE SHARES

Gotta love a code share. These are flights where two airlines cooperate to provide seats on a flight run by one of them. There will be only one name on the side of the aircraft, but maybe Qantas and British Airways or Virgin Atlantic and Delta Air Lines will each have their own flight codes for the journey. You may not know a thing about it until you turn up, unless you're savvy and look out for the four- (not three-) digit numerical codes that give the game away. It also really helps when you're checking in. These codeshares usually indicate that the airlines are all under the palm tree of global organisations like Star Alliance and Oneworld, which have frequent flier loyalty programmes attached. Great if you're a point plunderer. Not so great if you like the way a certain airline does things. The massive plus is that if there are four airlines code-sharing, you can check each of the names over the door for the best price. It might not be much, but there is sometimes a lag between operators. I've just tried it for a flight between Heathrow and Seattle. I saved a pound. OK, but still, a pound, eh? Not bad.

LIMBER UP, STAY FLEXIBLE

Quite apart from being a good way to avoid deep vein thrombosis, staying flexible helps you to save money in the long run. Many airlines now charge like a Trojan Warrior for even small changes, particularly to time and date. Buying a flexible ticket that allows you to change may cost a little more, but nowhere near as much as a new ticket after a missed connection. Yes, that is what insurance is for, but do you want to be sitting in Nairobi Airport making a claim on a mobile phone that's costing you a fortune, when you could just change your flight and relax? One shining example of a flexible fare is the offer

> *Buying a flexible ticket that allows you to change may cost a little more, but nowhere near as much as a new ticket after a missed connection.*

by easyJet which enables you to change flight dates and times after booking, for precisely zero pounds. Although restrictions apply, if you know you are travelling it's probably worth making an early purchase to adapt at your leisure later on.

EXTRA COSTS

There are some costs you will have to pay with every airline. These include air passenger duty, the UK Passenger Service Charge, an insurance and security levy that came in after 9/11 and the fuel surcharge. These should be incorporated into the price of the ticket, invisible, and never added after the event. Increasingly though, led by disruptors in the industry (and I'm looking at you, here, Ryanair) even really established airlines are starting to charge for whatever they can, notably seat allocation, baggage, priority boarding and food and drink. There are two ways to look at this. If it keeps the price of your flight down and is perfectly transparent, what's the problem? Why should you have to pay through your ticket for a meal you don't like when you can bring your own sandwiches? I get that bit. What I don't like one bit is the seat allocation thing.

Buy seats on a flight for you and your family and you might think it's a given that you'll all be in the same row. Not so! If you've got children to care for, or a vulnerable adult, the seating plan becomes not just a priority, but a necessity. I don't like it when you're forced to pay extra for things you can't avoid, but that's the way it's working out with many airlines. In 2017 the Civil Aviation Authority surveyed 4,000 people to find out about their flight seating issues. Just over half said they were told before they booked their flight that they would need to pay to ensure their group all sat together. That means that almost half were not. On the upside, around half of passengers who sat together did not have to pay to do so. For their part, airlines insist that seating plans are random. But charging for it is only one side of the story.

Understandably, the CAA are really concerned that this development among the airlines constitutes what always used to be called a surcharge – an unavoidable extra. They're trying to find a way to stop it. In the meantime, here's a really important bit of traveller power: All airlines are duty bound to keep children in the vicinity of their parents, to ensure any emergency evacuation is carried out swiftly and efficiently. If you're split up, this argument is the strongest arrow in your quiver, and don't hesitate to use it.

Matt Nav

Some airlines are notorious for splitting up travelling groups and there's even a suggestion it's not as random as you'd think. In 2017, *Watchdog* sponsored research of its own, sending groups of four people on four separate Ryanair flights. They discovered every single one was allocated a middle seat, which meant sitting apart from the rest of the group. Dr Jennifer Rogers, director of the Oxford University Statistical Consultancy, then calculated that the chances of all four people being randomly given middle seats was a stunning 1 in 540,000,000. In fact, those fliers were more likely to win the National Lottery, at 1 in 45,000,000, than be randomly allocated middle seats. Yet there they were, periodically bobbing up behind headrests to make contact with their travelling companions. While airlines insist there's nothing sinister in their seating plans it all stinks of a wonky algorithm at the very least.

TOP TIPS

Right, flight fans, here's a whistlestop tour of the things that can trip you up on your, erm, trip:

➜ Beware 24-hour clock and time-zone confusion. Double check that you don't buy a flight that leaves at 5am, then arrive at the airport ten hours after it's gone.

⬅ When you turn up for international travel, make sure you have your passport and that it has at least six months left to run before it is out of date, as some countries will insist upon it so they can get you out again.

➜ If you are going to Europe, go armed with your European Health Insurance Card (EHIC), which entitles you to receive medical treatment free of charge (for now) in EEA countries and Switzerland. The EHIC card is free and any site that promises to get one for a fee is trying to scam you. It is valid for UK citizens at least until the start of 2021.

⬅ Outside Europe check whether you need visas or vaccinations.

➜ Some countries need you to have the proper permit even if you are only transiting inside the airport. In America, you will need the Electronic System for Travel Authorisation (ESTA). It's an online application. Less famous is the electronic travel authorisation (eTA), which you need before you board a flight to Canada, even if you are only passing through.

← The Foreign and Commonwealth Office or National Health Service websites can advise on every destination. Don't forget to take all the paperwork for visas and vaccinations to the airport, or there's a risk it might not have been worth the pain and expense of having them. I've done it. Once. And no-one in my family has ever let me forget it.

OTHER PROTECTIONS

Even if you book flights and accommodation directly you might have ATOL protection. That's something that needs to be checked. But you may well be safe under the ABTA umbrella. ABTA can also act as arbiters between disgruntled tourists and holiday providers. AITO, the specialist travel association, also provides a safety net if you buy one of its holidays. And of course if you don't now buy your holiday with a credit card to get Section 75 protection (see p. 23), then we simply cannot be friends any more.

DELAYS, CANCELLATIONS AND LOST LUGGAGE

Where there are flights, there are delays. The good news is that an EU rule means you are entitled to compensation if you are delayed for more than two hours or your flight is cancelled. If it's cancelled, you should receive a refund within 7 days – and despite what some airlines might say, COVID-19 doesn't change that. Specifically, it's EU regulation 261/2004 that you need to quote, which was adopted in 2005. Although the UK has left the EU, it's thought this arrangement will continue, although at this stage, quite frankly, who knows? It's only applicable to EU-regulated flights. That means a flight that's departed from an EU airport, no matter what flag the aircraft's flying, or one that's landed in one of the 27 countries that comprise the EU, plus Iceland, Liechtenstein, Norway and Switzerland. And the reason for the delay must lie with the airline, so bad weather or industrial action by air traffic controllers won't cut it.

Absent crew or strikes by airline staff are deemed to be within an airline's control. Crucially, you must have arrived at your destination more than two hours late to receive financial help. If you've suffered a long wait in departures but a powerful tail wind has you landing earlier than expected, check the timings carefully because the two-hour margin is key. The compensations starts at €250 and goes up depending on the length of

> *The compensations starts at €250 and goes up depending on the length of delay and the length of flight.*

Matt Stat

Around a quarter of all flights are delayed by 15 minutes or more, according to claimcompass.eu. The main reasons? Air Traffic Control and weather, followed by bird strikes. You see, pigeons have a very strong trade union indeed.

delay and the length of flight. You're also entitled to food and drink and a couple of telephone calls, and a hotel room if the delay goes on.

As you can imagine, this compensation is very expensive, and airlines will do anything they can to avoid it. It's really important that you find out exactly why you've been delayed as soon as possible, and don't be fobbed off. Any evidence you can gather from staff could help in the claim you'll put in later on, so take notes with names attached. If your claim gets turned down, turn to the CAA for help. Keep any receipts for expenses you've incurred. You could stick them on the pile for the compensation claim.

For other parts of the world, check to see if similar compensation schemes are in place, complain to the airline and study the t's and c's on your travel insurance. Some will offer (limited) compensation.

The Montreal Convention, ratified by an impressive 120 countries, can help with any costs incurred after a flight cancellation or some lost baggage. If you get time in the pre-holiday rush, take pics of your bag and contents to verify any future claim made under the Montreal Convention. Although the time limit is seven days, it makes better sense to begin the claim before you leave the airport. After 21 days your bag is officially lost. You can get full compensation. This replaces the far less glamorous Warsaw Convention, which paid out a pittance based on the weight of whatever got lost, perhaps harking back to the time when people regularly took house bricks with them on holiday.

Matt Nav

When an airline says last call, take 'em seriously. As we've seen, big fines come crashing down on airlines if they don't fly in on time, and my best friend, a long-haul pilot, says passenger punctuality is a big problem. No surprises that a few years ago easyJet introduced their 'if you're late, we won't wait' policy, and enforced it rigorously. Rumour has it that a very famous television personality didn't take this promise seriously enough, and arrived for his flight to Ireland after the retractable barrier had been pulled across. 'Do you know who I am?' came the legendary question. Quick as a whip, the employee at the gate opened the tannoy. 'Ladies and gentlemen, do we have a doctor in the house? There is a gentleman here who, despite holding a passport in his right hand, doesn't appear to know who he is.'

AIRPORT PARKING

Was this always a thing? Handing over your car keys to a stranger at the airport, only to fly away and not worry about it, because, you know, that's what everyone does these days, right? Not to mention the fact that there are loads of pictures of fences and CCTV cameras on the website. Tcha! It'll be fine. And anyway... I'm in Cuba!

I'm sorry to report that airport parking is one of those boom industries for rogue traders right now. They just can't get enough of it. We've seen cars returned damaged, filthy, with mystery miles racked up, speeding and parking fines, and in some cases, not returned at all. Here are a few tips to keep your car safe:

➜ Choose a reputable company, preferably one that is approved by the airport itself and is a member of the International Parking Community and the British Parking Association.

⬅ Pre-book to get best prices.

➜ Don't leave any valuables in the car, in case it's not left parked in a secure area.

⬅ If in any doubt at all, book through the airport's own website.

Matt Nav

We had the most hilarious time on *Rogue Traders* with an airport parking company who had simply hired a farmer's field near Gatwick for a month and stuck a load of cars in it. In itself, not illegal, it turns out, but they weren't being totally honest with their customers when they booked through a website. The keys to the cars, including Porsches and Maseratis, were all kept in the boot of another car, which itself was unlocked and accessible. The field was open on all sides, and was a regular haunt for dog walkers and, bizarrely, investigative television journalists with their camera crew. The question naturally occurred to us: what would happen if we, having left our car with them, simply decided to come into that field and drive it away again? Answer: nothing. No sirens, no flashing lights, not even a call to the police. The employees watched us driving away as if it were the most natural thing in the world. Their defence? They never claimed it was secure parking. OK!

Accommodation

HOTELS

Why don't you staaaay, just a little bit longer?

Well, because, in many cases, the room you book is not up to scratch, for a start. We used to get our information about holiday accommodation through brochures, peering at tiny thumbnail pictures of a room which ceased to look like that as soon as the photographer left. Alternatively, in the heady days of Teletext, we wouldn't even see the rooms we were booking. How trusting we were!

Online travel agencies should have put all that worry to bed, as it were. OTAs like Expedia, Tripadvisor and Booking.com can supply you with an almost endless stream of hi-res pictures of beautifully folded towels. And whatever they're doing, it works. 81 per cent of holidays are now booked online.

Their comparison sites do the heavy lifting when it comes to giving you options while the curated reviews help you decide on a hotel or villa. Now, as with all online reviews, they are to be taken with a dash of Angostura bitters. Read a few and you'll see there is an over-representation of the extremes. We know that despite their best efforts, illicit advertising and vendetta reviews still get through. Where you want to look is somewhere between 2 and 4 stars, where people have taken time to think about what they're writing. You'll get a much better flavour of the place you're calling home for week or two. Star rating systems are also worthy of a healthy pinch of seasoning. They vary hugely from one country to the next, and often relate to things you may never need. A sewing kit or shoe polish can bump you up into the next bracket. It really won't tell you anything about the quietness of your room, helpfulness of the staff or ease of parking – the things we really care about. Work out what matters to you, and treat the stars as the very loosest of indications that a place will make you happy.

The hotel industry has been turned on its head by this tsunami of OTAs. Just like the first package holiday operators, these companies not only buy accommodation in bulk but charge commission to hotels, to the joy of consumers who like the instant reward of knowing they've got the best price. Or have they?

Where you want to look is somewhere between 2 and 4 stars, where people have taken time to think about what they're writing.

Some of the big hotel chains are a bit fed up with the OTAs, because they've meant hotels who haven't landed the custom themselves miss out on advantages like repeat bookings, upselling opportunities and the chance to foster brand loyalty. Some of them have been trying to reverse the tide and are taking on the OTAs at their own game.

You'll often find best price guarantees, loyalty benefits and upgrades aplenty if you book directly through one of the big chains. It's all because they want to take the power (and the commission) out of the hands of the online crew. All of this is travel industry shenanigans until you know what it means for you: get the OTA price (or a number of them) and cross-check it against the hotel's best offer. And then...

HAGGLE, Marvin! Come out of the red corner swinging! You may not get much change out of the OTA, but you should be able to deliver a few uppercuts to the hotel-direct booking price, particularly if they offer price-matching or best price guarantees. And don't forget that prices can change over time. If you can take the flexible option and cancel when a cheaper price becomes available, do it! And bob! And weave! Jab, jab, jab!

Some hotels offer a pricing option that's cheaper if you commit to the room there and then. That's all very well until the price plummets and ends up being cheaper still. So consider paying a higher price from the get go, one that allows you to cancel at the last minute, so you can scrap that first booking and make a second at the lower price.

SHORT-TERM HOLIDAY LETS

Shall we talk Airbnb? Let's! Or, more precisely, short-term holiday lets. Someone's actual flat, house or bedroom that can work out much, much cheaper, not to say more interesting, than a hotel room. When it started it was a guerrilla disruptor of a business, formed when the owners pumped up a lilo in their front room and called it a place to stay. Now the business has been inflated beyond all recognition, with a revenue of $2.6 billion a year (as of 2017). Wow, cool, right?

Yes, but it might have been pumped up a little too quickly. There have been horror stories. Some host homes have been used for parties, as brothels and as drug dens. Some guests have experienced assault, discrimination and cash demands, or found hidden cameras. Everyone accepts that the bad experiences are in the minority, but they still count. The most solid advice from travel experts around Airbnb is to be led by reviews and to only use official Airbnb channels for communication and payment. It limits the potential for fraudsters to make cash on the site, which isn't the only 'spare room' platform in operation. In addition, the Airbnb empires some people have built up have been ripped apart by COVID-19's months of lockdown emptiness. It has certainly shaken confidence in the model.

So, to Airbnb or not to Airbnb? Well, it is fun and can be cheap, but watch out for sketchy pics and prices that look too cheap for the area. Your go-to tool should be the reverse image search. Google do one. Copy the main pic into the search engine and see what comes up. If it's a stock photo, or doesn't match the address you've been given, let it go, let it go etc.

Matt Nav

See how they run! Run their dodgy Airbnb-based lettings business, that is. We got wind of a company that was running a load of really nice-looking holiday rentals through Airbnb, all based in Central and West London. This was the second generation of providers – not homestays, but a small business with an office, box of keys and staff. The problem was that, on arrival, the customer was kept hanging around in the office while keys were sought, and guess what? Rather than that lovely little mansion block overlooking Hyde Park, they were transported a mile and a half up the Edgware Road to a dingy old dive and then left there. For many visitors it was their first experience of London, being stuck out on a limb without a clue where they were. We tried the service ourselves, and got the same treatment, so I strolled into the offices of the firm on the Edgware Road to find the owner of the business… and boy could he move! I reckon we did a sub-4 minute mile until my cameraman begged for mercy and we stopped to get him an oxygen mask. Beware!

COMPLAINING

Complaining about a holiday is a bit special, so it's worth talking about it here. It's not like a washing machine or a car. Once you've left the resort, you can't go back and gather evidence.

Package travellers

Got a smart phone? Use it! Take pictures of whatever's bothering you, whether it's pests, leaks or workmen under your balcony. And take notes too: when the thing happened, who was involved. You'll need this to back up your story. Next, speak to your rep. They'll be the ones who can fix whatever's wrong fastest. Like all complaints, get them on your side. If it's happening to more than one of you, get together to give your case strength, but without looking like you're ganging up. You want to help them do their job as well as possible. If your rep can't help, get in contact with their head office back home (if they're UK based). Go as high up the chain as you can, one step at a time, until you get satisfaction.

If they're members, think about contacting ABTA while you're in the resort. They can put pressure on the operator to resolve things while you're still there. Definitely preferable to some form of compensation after the event

– it's never enough to compensate for the time you've wasted on your one holiday of the year. Don't accept vouchers unless it's really trivial. If they've let you down once, why would you book with them again?

Make your complaint chronological and logical. As always, stay calm and polite, and encourage the company to see your side

> *Go as high up the chain as you can, one step at a time, until you get satisfaction.*

of things. Angry loses you points, always. If you have the acting skills to pull off fainting, though, give it a go. It's a deal-breaker (joke).

Only go for redress that matches your distress. There was a suspicion early in my *Watchdog* days that some holidaymakers were using the compensation system as their own lottery win. Don't be that guy. That guy is a bad guy. If all else fails, try the small claims court, a relatively simple but time-consuming process which, if you're serious about it, can bring results.

Holiday sickness

Why does being somewhere sunny sometimes hit your tummy? Well, because germs like to go on holiday too. They positively come alive in the heat. India, Kenya and Thailand regularly top the charts for bugging out tourists.

The tiny tourists having fun in your body come from a number of different sources. Food preparation and cooking or a poor hygiene regime in the swimming pool can give you any one of salmonella, E. coli, cryptosporidium, norovirus, campylobacter and Shigella dysentery.

If you suffer from a problem like this on holiday you will need to see a doctor and get the appropriate treatments. Don't forget to keep receipts so you can make a case to your tour operator – and be aware that some illnesses won't manifest themselves until after you get home.

There are some steps you can take to help yourself:

➡ Take a first aid kit

⬅ Drink plenty of water, and make it bottled if the tap water isn't safe

➡ Avoid alcohol

⬅ Wash your hands frequently

➡ Stay out of the sun during the hottest hours of the day

⬅ Use sunscreen, a hat and sunglasses by the pool

➡ Put on insect repellent on top of sunscreen

⬅ Wear long-sleeved tops and trousers to avoid insect bites

➡ Make a note of emergency numbers in the vicinity

Matt Nav

Brits abroad have gone and got themselves a bit of a reputation for insurance scams. After 2013 there was a 500 per cent rise in the number of compensation claims against tour operators for holiday sickness, with holidaymakers being encouraged to ask for cash before they even leave the resort by lurking claims management company operatives. In 2017 one big tour operator compared the illness claims put in by the British in the summer months – just under 4,000 – to those put in by the Germans – 114 – and the Scandinavians – 39.

However, European hoteliers have launched a counter offensive in the 'gastroenteritis wars' (not catchy – should have been Battle of the Bugs), asking visitors to report any sickness immediately so that a stool sample can be taken to provide the necessary evidence of sickness. If that's not enough to make you feel better quickly, one Greek hotel began a counter-claim against a British couple who sued, amounting to £170,000, for defamation, while in Spain anyone found guilty of a fraudulent claim risks a three-year jail sentence.

Look at me! I'm healed! Just like that!

DRIVING A HIRE CAR ABROAD

Well, now. Here we open a veritable Pandora's box of scamduggery and dodgepottedness. It's all bound up in the fact that you're driving around someone else's car in a foreign country, you see. Thousands of pounds of liability, rules you don't understand, a foreign language. For a shady desk jockey in search of commission, it's like shooting very large fish in a tiny barrel. Let's look at what you have to provide first:

➡ You will need your licence and a licence check code, which you can get from DVLA with your driving licence number, your national insurance number and the post code on your driving licence.

⬅ You might need an International Driving Permit, which are available from the post office, and a portable kit that includes items like spare light bulbs and breathalysers, but check to see the rules that apply in the country in which you will be driving. Those items may not necessarily come with the hire car so take them if you can.

Right. Now we get to the first bit that can go horribly wrong. Fuel from a pump is usually clearly price tagged.

You'll know how much you're paying per litre. Return your hire car anything other than completely full, and you could find that price doubles or trebles.

Then we're on to insurance. You may not know it to look at them, but that agent handing you your keys (eventually) is a salesperson. A big chunk of their take-home comes from selling you extras, and the biggest one of these is insurance. Collision damage waiver, super collision damage waiver, personal effects protection, carefree personal protection – all of these may get fired your way, and most you should dodge like Keanu Reeves dodges bullets.

Upgrades! Who doesn't love an upgrade? More room to stretch out, stick another bag in the boot. Well, don't assume that upgrade is free. And don't assume you're being told the cost for the whole period. We've heard of cases where it's the daily rate you're told, only to face a huge bill at the end of the trip.

One answer to this is to arrange any extras you might need – including insurance, sat navs, child seats, etc. through the website when you book. It should, and I'm going to underline should, mean fewer surprises when you land at Paloma Blanca International after a six-hour flight. Not the best time to be negotiating.

> Don't assume that upgrade is free.

The most important bit

When returning your car, while there's daylight, take pictures of everything you can before handing the keys back. Do this with the check-in person if you can, and get their 'OK, no problem' and full name before you hit duty free. Just like hire-car fuel, hire-car repairs are carried out in a palace, by supermodels with golden tools, and are therefore incredibly expensive. A big, big way to rake it in.

For disputes that arise with car hire on the continent there's the European car rental conciliation service scheme (ECRCS). I've never tried them, but I bet it's not as easy as not getting scammed in the first place.

Matt Nav

We'd seen stories for ages about some of Europe's biggest car hire companies taking the mickey. The Competition and Markets Authority agreed – in 2015, they forced a series of commitments out of Avis Budget, Enterprise, Hertz, Sixt and Europcar to improve their business, including giving a total price at the beginning of the process, and clear info about extras. If a firm sells to UK customers, it has to abide by UK law, in this case the CPFUT (see p.16). No excuses.

TRAINS

If you understand Britain's byzantine train ticketing system you are probably a worthy contestant on University Challenge. You might even stand a chance of getting there on time. There's nothing simple about buying tickets, but here's a starter for ten!

After 1995 the railways were run by some 20 private operators, each with their own foibles. But they are co-ordinated as National Rail, so buying tickets and finding information should be easier. So the first place to check out railway journeys is on www.nationalrail.co.uk, a site backed by the Rail Delivery Group on behalf of train companies.

If you are booking ahead, what's known as off-peak or anytime fares start appearing 12 weeks before the day of travel. Basically, the first restricts you to travelling outside commuter hours while the second can take you at any time – and has a price tag to match. But don't jump too soon. These are the pricier cousins of the advance fare, which comes out some two to four weeks later. If you make an enquiry before these have appeared, set an email alert that will tell you when the cheaper tickets you want are released. About a million advance tickets are used each week. Cheaper they may be, but advance tickets are inflexible and do restrict you to certain trains. You could

> *Cheaper they may be, but advance tickets are inflexible and do restrict you to certain trains.*

incur a fine if you try to game the system by using any other. Miss your train and you've lost your money.

Generally speaking, there are cheap off-peak times and not-so-cheap ones too. It's much cheaper to travel on a Wednesday lunchtime than a Friday evening. In fact, most services attract a different charge, although a search engine will usually help you to find the best price.

However, that software is trying to find you the quickest journey. Among the search results look for the button that asks you to click for slower routes with cheaper fares. It should present a long list for you to probe.

You can buy tickets with individual rail companies, at sites like thetrainline.com, which charges a booking fee, or with raileurope.co.uk, which doesn't. That should be the main difference in the prices, but I've seen that some sites don't list all possible routes, so there may well be price differences too.

Ticket splitting

Can you do the splits? I bet you can! Split ticketing involves dividing your journey into a few smaller journeys, and buying individual tickets to cover each of those legs. Shorter journeys work out cheaper per mile, and the savings can be impressive over a long journey, but a few rules to stick to:

→ The train MUST stop at the stations you've got on your tickets.

← DON'T get out. It will make for a very long journey indeed.

→ Get ready to move about. You'll have different seat reservations with each leg.

With a ticket splitting website you can buy the journey in one go, in much the same way as any other. Don't forget that seat reservations with all tickets are free.

Railcards

There are annual railcards that will save you a third of journey costs, if you have a regular travelling companion, are under 30, a pensioner or have disabilities. The cost of the card is usually recouped on its first outing. For hardened train travellers there are season tickets, which usually provide a discount although the cost of one can be prohibitive.

Delays

Trains seem just as prone to delays as planes. You remember those 20-odd train companies mentioned a few paragraphs back? Each has its own passenger charter which sets out its approach to compensation when trains are delayed, but most will play by the rules set by the national Delay Repay scheme, which guarantees compensation if you arrive more than or, in some cases, 30 minutes late. Individual charters are downloadable from the National Rail website.

TRAVEL INSURANCE

Right, so let me be honest: I've NEVER taken out the insurance that's bundled in with a holiday.

If you're booking through a travel agent they might make you feel like you have to have it, or add it to the bill without your permission, or even say there's a charge if you don't take it. Naughty, naughty travel agents! You can't do that! It's illegal upselling under the terms of the CPFUT regs of 2008, and if they carry on then there will be hell to pay, Just wait 'til your father gets home.

But holiday insurance is essential for most overseas trips. However unlikely it may seem, the costs of a repatriation for medical reasons can be as much as a house purchase. It's also worth asking who's going to help you if your money or cards get stolen in a country where you know no-one and don't speak the language. A death in the family, a house fire, a redundancy, an unexpected pregnancy or a call for jury service – all of these will have you changing your plans. One in every 20 travellers makes a claim on insurance and by far the most are made for cancellations.

So where to go? OK, we're back knocking at the door of the comparison sites, but don't forget some insurers don't feature on them, and don't make a judgement on price alone – SDCD. Compare cover before you compare price. Millions of pounds of cover are what you want for all the big stuff like medical and repatriation. Don't forget to mention any medical issues you might have in advance. It might not affect your premium as much as you think, but failure to mention it is a great reason for insurers to wriggle out of paying you. Medical is the reason the cost of travel insurance goes up with age. It's the biggest cost and, of course, your risk of getting ill increases with age. But car insurance gets cheaper! So, you know, swings and roundabouts! There are specialist insurers for older travellers, which might not show up on every comparison site.

Luxury items over a certain value might be excluded from your policy. If you're taking your tiara to the beach, make sure you've let your insurer know. Equally, you might have some sort of holiday cover for your stuff if you've got household contents insurance. No point paying twice for the same thing, so choose less or no cover if you can. Monthly-fee bank accounts can come with travel insurance as part of their bundled benefits (see p. 134).

If you take more than one holiday a year, even just within the UK, it's really worth considering an annual multi-trip insurance policy for you and your family. Not sure if you have a family? Just check down the back of seats in your car! Find half a biscuit or an action figure? Well, then, you've got yourself a family, my friend! Having year-round insurance also means you're covered as soon as you book your trip. If COVID-19 has taught us anything, it's that you're best to insure as soon as you book, or before.

Take your travel insurance policy with you on holiday, and separately, in a sealed plastic wallet, take your policy number alongside the telephone number you need to make a claim. If there's a problem, keep receipts for any expenses incurred. Also, try to get your insurer to agree medical treatment before it's carried out. You may well have to pay up front for any hospital treatment you receive. If items are lost or stolen, report them to the local police within 24 hours. Holiday nightmares are few and far between – but at least now you are prepared.

> *If you're taking your tiara to the beach, make sure you've let your insurer know.*

chapter
eleven

Complaining: How to Fight Your Corner and Win

It's all very well me banging on about your rights under law, and getting what's due to you. When it comes down to it, I can't be with you when you need me, and no-one is going to help you out of a fix and save your money from going down the pan unless you do it yourself. At least in the first instance, you're going to have to draw it to someone's attention that something's gone wrong. Welcome to the subtle but essential art of the complaint. You will need a pen and some paper!

First, let's start with a bit of roleplay. With the people you love, you've gathered at a restaurant for a special occasion but the meal takes ages to appear and when it finally arrives, it's cold. You're disappointed and it's an expensive meal. Do you:

a) rage at the waiting staff until your forehead vein throbs

b) talk menacingly about your 'particular skills' acquired over a 'very long career making consumer investigative television' that make you 'a nightmare' for eateries like this

c) eat your cold food, pay the bill, leave the restaurant and pretend it never happened. Cry a bit every day for the next week

d) none of the above

I'm hoping you picked d). Letting things slide as in c) means that you lose self-respect and the respect of those around you, and the restaurant has lost a vital opportunity to improve what it does. Similarly, b) shows that you are a bit of a knob, and prepares everyone in the restaurant for a battle which takes time and is likely to benefit no-one. I suspect that if you chose a) then you may have problems which need addressing elsewhere in your life. I'm not saying that you're a bad person, just that you tend to do bad things. Sort it out.

> *A complaint is not necessarily a bad thing.*

So let's talk about d). What does d) look like? Well, in short, you're looking for the best possible outcome, requiring the least effort from you, and, if possible, allowing both sides of the complaint to feel like they're got something useful from the experience. I know that's not necessarily the way you'll look at complaints right now, but it's absolutely the way forward from now on. A complaint is not necessarily a bad thing. It's a chance for you to get the product or service you want, and for the provider to learn about how they can improve that thing. Win, win. Include me on the deal and it's win, win, win.

On the record

During a complaint, make sure you are getting everything down on paper or a digital device as it happens. Time and date, full name of counterpart, along with their role. It's legal to record phone calls as long as you don't reveal the contents to a third party. The easiest way to organise this is to have a day book: a log of every conversation you have, as you have it. It's much easier than trying to recreate the moment weeks or months later, and being able to show a timeline with other events around it could help as evidence.

Check yourself

… before you wreck yourself. First things first: is your complaint really valid? We can all be swayed by feelings of embarrassment or loss in the moment, but you must be honest about how much of the problem you could have avoided if you'd behaved differently, perhaps better. Did someone try to explain that, for instance, your energy would be supplied on a standard variable rate once the fixed deal expired? Or that this product is not really suitable for dry skin? There's a good chance that in our busy lives we may have missed something important that was said to us or contained in the contract that we signed. Having a good think back through telephone calls (recorded for training purposes…) and a skim through any paperwork you may have will save you a lot of bother and, possibly, a Himalayan climb-down later in the process. I've done it. Plate, knife and fork, words. Now eat those words.

> There's a good chance that in our busy lives we may have missed something important that was said to us.

Matt Nav

That's not to say that just because you've been told
something was wrong, you have to accept it. Terms
contained in very small print in a contract, or delivered
without time to change your mind, are often used
as a get-out by companies trying to pull a fast one.
An airport parking company we featured on *Rogue
Traders* (see p. 354) handed over a piece of paper as we
handed over our keys which stated 'your car may be
parked in a field'. Unlikely you're going to do anything
at that point, as you're about to check in and check
out for a fortnight. Unfair. The legal proof of small
print is that it must be written in plain English and easy
to understand. The key is that you must have been
given a chance to understand, and time to change your
decision based on the facts you've been given.

The nub of the matter

Why are you peed off? What exactly is demonstrably wrong with the deal you've got? This can't be about your feelings. What you need is to be able to show, with evidence, how what you've ended up with deviates from what you were promised. What you were promised can be made up of:

→ Obligations under law / terms in a written contract

← What you were told verbally by salespeople or other staff

→ Content of advertisements prior to purchase

← Accepted legal standards for the thing you've bought (edible food, roadworthy cars)

→ Generally accepted standards for the thing you've bought which weren't explicitly excluded from your deal (holiday insurance that covers personal possessions, for example)

← Things you've had from this supplier before which have been changed without notice

→ Their company policies, which again, can't change without notice. These include guidelines issued by trade bodies to which they're signed up, under the CPFUTR 2008

There may be more than one thing that's wrong. Make a list of all of them, with the most serious at the top. That's the order in which these need to be tackled.

Impact

How has this all affected you? Have you had to take days off work? Buy a different service or product at personal expense? Have you had to arrange childcare? Have you had to hire a car or paid for a hotel stay? Keep receipts for any out-of-pocket expenses. Now we can come to have a look at your feelings, but only inasmuch as they are relevant. Will this affect your decision to choose this company again? Would you recommend them to your friends? These are important ideas to get across as they represent pound signs floating out of the window for the firm.

What do you want?

OK, so let's say that, in an ideal world, you can get whatever you want out of this process. What does that look like? And is that realistic? Let's say your holiday has been cancelled because it turns out that the holiday company has overbooked your accommodation. How can they realistically make that right? You'd be entitled to a refund, of course, but are you going to be able to book somewhere at this late stage? And are they in the position to offer something better than you had before?

If they move you from a four-star to a five-star hotel in a different resort, does that make up for the fact it wasn't your first choice?

Having an idea of what you want from this process is really important. It's telling the company you're dealing with that you understand not just your legal rights, but also what your time and effort are worth, and that their mistake or muck-up has a price, which you as the wronged party are setting. It can be a refund, a replacement, compensation, or just a simple 'sorry'. It's also important for you, psychologically, to know what you want. Of course, what you can achieve might be dictated by legal recourse – what the law says you can have. Nevertheless, set a realistic goal and stick to it. And don't be greedy, because no-one likes that guy, and, in all likelihood, you will fail.

> *Having an idea of what you want from this process is really important.*

First contact

OK! Notebook and pencil at the ready. So you know what you went wrong, and you know what you want. It's time to get back in contact with the company. Don't wait too long. It's better to get something brief but accurate in early rather than waiting weeks to fashion exactly the correct form of words. This first contact is crucial, because it sets the tone for everything that follows. Put ridiculously simply, you stand the best chance of rubbing out this problem if you are an ERASER:

Empathetic
Reasonable
Assertive
Supported
Evidenced
Relentless

Let's go through these one by one.

EMPATHETIC

Every customer service operative is also a customer. They are just like you. Hard to believe from the end of the phone, but all of them, on their lunch hour, nip to the shops and buy a sandwich, go online to look at sofas, and take out car insurance, all of which they want to be SQUAD Fit for Life, just like you. Bear this in mind as you call them, being positive about their company wherever possible and using their first name wherever appropriate, and using simple techniques which demonstrate that you understand their side of things. Say things like:

→ 'Paul, I've really enjoyed being your customer for years.'

← 'I bet you have a lot of customers who call about this.'

→ 'I hate to be the one who has to point this out.'

← 'You must be sick of people calling about this sort of thing.'

For managers:

→ 'I really think there's a way to improve what you do here.'

← 'I think it's important that you get this fixed, for your own good.'

But empathy is a two-way street. There's a good chance that they regard you just as the 27th customer service call they've had to take this morning. Don't be a number. Make sure you're appealing to their humanity and common sense as well:

→ 'It would be so much better if I could get this sorted quickly. I've got loads to do.'

← 'Could you help me get this resolved?'

→ 'I really need your help.'

I also find that if you ask a few empathetic questions, especially later on in the process, when you're struggling to get results, it can be pretty powerful:

→ 'I'd ask you to consider how you'd respond if you were in my shoes.'

← 'Do you think it's fair that X has happened?'

→ 'How do you think this reflects on (company name) right now?'

← 'Would you sign up for this deal?'

And then…

… leave a silence.

Silence is the great secret weapon in the complaint phone call. As complainers, we are expected to fill every available gap with rage and retribution. By not being that person, you're allowing them to be you for a short while, to consider your position, and taking the pressure off, so that they can come up with a solution for you. Above all, it gives you the unmistakable air of being…

REASONABLE

Open, approachable, logical, honest, fair. All of these, but above all, willing to listen to reason from the other side, and not closed to the idea of compromise. It's in your voice, the words and phrases you use, the ideas for resolution that you propose, and the timing of your contacts with the other side (five before lunch? Too many). All of these should paint a picture of someone who wants a resolution quickly – the same thing they will want, unless they are an out-and-out dodgepot (see 'dodgepots', p. 393). Being reasonable is great. It's not the same as being a pushover. That's why you must be...

ASSERTIVE

We're not being pushed around here. We are stating our case clearly. Because of stages 1 and 2, we know that something has gone wrong, and we know what we need to happen to fix it. There is no need to apologise for these things, or be fobbed off. Speak in clear tones, making sure you're being understood, and at the end of every contact, make sure you set and understand the timeframe for whatever happens next, whether it's a refund, further correspondence or a conversation. You're writing all this down, remember, so that you can hold them to it later, but don't forget you should also have a record on your phone (or phone bill for a landline) of every call you've made to the company, and a good record of the important bits of that phone call.

> *Going over someone's head is only really useful when you feel they no longer have the power to give you what you want.*

SUPPORTED

You are not alone. Even if you feel like it, you're not. Wherever possible, demonstrate that you are speaking with other people or agencies who are overseeing the process and who will, unless justice is done, fly to your rescue whenever you climb the stairs to the roof and project the bat signal. These can include ombudsmen, Citizens Advice, *Which?* magazine, Shelter (if it's housing), your MP, Trading Standards, the police (only if you think it's a criminal matter) and of course, the country's longest-running consumer programme, all of us here at *Watchdog* and *Rogue Traders*. If you think your complaint is something that the company's own management might want to know about, then also copy in members of their board, although realise that by doing so, you're breaching your bond of trust and empathy with the individual that you're dealing with. Going over someone's head is only really useful when you feel they no longer have the power to help you get what you want.

EVIDENCED

From the earliest opportunity – your first call – make it clear that you have got your evidence stacked up. You know what was promised, and you've got evidence of how what you've got is not that. Demonstrate that you know which laws or company policies have been broken. If you've got something really specific – for instance from the CPFUTR 2008 (see p. 16), then that's your trump card. But don't come on like Hercule Poirot unveiling a murderer. You're bringing this to their attention so that you can put it right together. Lay out your grievances in order of seriousness and provability. Ideally, you want the first one to be the most important, and based on rock-solid evidence. It means you can keep coming back to it as often as you like, as your starting and ending point. Keep a record of everything you can, and be aware that a conversation with a customer service bod isn't just a chance for you to get your point across: it can also add to your pile of evidence. Take special note of phrases that sound a bit like:

→ 'You're the third person today with this problem.'

← 'Yes, it's a recognised fault.'

→ 'They started issuing replacements but now they're just doing repairs.'

← 'They're being recalled in other countries but not here.'

All of these indicate there's a bigger problem which they're trying to keep hidden. Stick it in the notebook for later use. There's nothing more satisfying in a complaint than using the phrase 'I note from my conversation with Davina on 11/03/2019 that this is a recognised problem'. Not great for Davina, but at the end of the day, it's not her decision to be all cloak and dagger about a problem with 30,000 fridges whose doors won't shut. Remember that a received email gives you a timed record of your conversations, which you won't get from a phone call. It also gives you the chance, by CCing people in, to write to more than one person at a time, none of whom can claim they haven't seen it – especially if you ask for an automatic receipt when it's been opened. Don't write pages and pages unless it's been requested. Important people send short emails, because they know that most people don't have the attention span to get past the first couple of paragraphs.

RELENTLESS

We never give up. If they don't stick to the time frame, don't let them get away with it, and keep going. Persistence (ERASEP? No.) is key. A steady, constant stream of reminders to the company that you're not going anywhere is far more effective than a flash-in-the-pan explosion of anger and resentment. Picture yourself as the big machine that dug the Channel Tunnel, grinding out a journey towards the light. Imagine the longest that your complaint could possibly take to get resolved, and then double it. You're in for the long haul, and let anything else be a blessed surprise. Devote a couple of hours a week, no more, for as long as it takes. The long arc of history bends towards justice.

You're an Olympic endurance athlete. Event: Complaining. You **will** take the gold.

The escalation game

If your first contact doesn't yield results, as I've hinted, you'll have to move this thing onwards and upwards. You need to find the limits of what the person you're speaking to can achieve, and when you've reached those limits, find the person who can do more. The computer may say no, but the computer is not in charge here. Take full names, and politely but firmly ask who is in charge of what they do. You're working from the bottom up, but this is also a good time to find out who's at the top of the tree. Find out the names of CEOs and chairpeople. They may have a presence on social media platforms such as Twitter, Facebook, Instagram or the business networking site LinkedIn. You can often work out their email addresses by reverse-engineering those of the people you're already talking to. You can use these

> *The computer may say no, but the computer is not in charge here.*

contacts to bring pressure on their underlings to act, or at least know that they can't get away with utter nonsense. It's key not to let these contacts add up to some form of threat, though. Just like the greedy complainer, no-one likes that person, and it can result in a shutdown of your complaint. Be an ERASER here or you're the one that will be rubbed out. Don't forget that the reputation of the company is at stake, and that, up to a certain point, you both have the same goal: to make things better for their customers, one of whom just happens to be you.

Social media

Many firms now deal with an element of their customer service response on social media platforms. A double-edged sword, because there's an element of airing your dirty washing in public, but that openness does achieve a couple of things. It genuinely offers customers a means of redress. I've seen things get fixed very quickly. It also sets a precedent, showing customers what they can expect from the company if they have similar problems. A roadmap for complaining, if you like. I think it's a big step forward, and the bods who man social media customer care are brave people. They can score pretty big by getting it right though, making their firm look human and empathetic. They can also get it horribly wrong by flooding our timelines with ads and then failing to respond to criticism when it crops up.

Matt Nav

Social media fails by big companies' accounts are pretty rife. From US Airways inadvertently tweeting filthy pics, to Adidas congratulating those who 'survived' the Boston Marathon, the ease of sharing sometimes results in some pretty impressive meltdowns. Possibly my favourite so far is the moment when music seller HMV went on a cost-cutting exercise without first securing its customer-facing Twitter account. 'We're tweeting live from HR, where we're all being fired! Exciting!' read one post. 'Mass execution of loyal employees who love the brand!', another. One of the downsides, it appears, of giving your firm a human face, is that it often requires actual, unpredictable and emotional humans to be involved, in all their glory.

Matt Stat

Around half the CEOs of FTSE 350 and S&P 500 listed companies have a presence on social media. They're not big posters though – only 25 per cent post once in a year. Slightly fewer are on LinkedIn.

Wait 'til your father gets home

Do you suspect that your strongly worded letter of complaint has been binned? Are your calls and tweets getting you nowhere? You should have dropped big hints by now that you've got other resources to turn to if need be. If you're still not getting the result you feel is right, it's time to invoke them now. Many industries have an ombudsman and you can escalate your complaint to them. There are also various trade bodies and industry watchdogs keen to see fair play, to maintain the reputation of their sector. Your adversary may even be signed up to them. A bit of detective work on the internet will track them down, or contact Citizens Advice for further direction. When you fear the law has been breached try Trading Standards, which is charged with keeping business honest and safe. You can get the media involved if you want to. I hear some of them are OK, but their real strength is letting others know what's going on so that they can avoid it.

Dodgepots

The advice so far is all based on a scenario where you are on the other end of a complaint with someone who gives a monkey's. Of course, that's making a bit of an assumption. At some point in your life you'll find yourself in a wrangle with someone who, for whatever reason, has nothing to lose, or does not care about the reputation of their firm. This may be because they do not intend to continue with this firm long-term, operate from a mobile phone in a van, or are adept at shape-shifting and phoenixing every 18 months into another company name. There is obviously no point in appealing to someone's better side in these circumstances. You will be banging your head against a wall. So what motivates dodgepots? How can we get anything – a refund, repair, replacement or apology – from someone whose aim in life is to avoid censure and carry on laughing at those of us unlucky enough to be involved with them?

> *At some point in your life you'll find yourself in a wrangle with someone who, for whatever reason, has nothing to lose*

Well, the first thing is to establish that you're not dealing with someone who values Bona Fides – the idea of acting in good faith. If you get no sense that they are concerned about your complaint – a failure to engage, a series of excuses concerning personal injury or family bereavement – then read the writing on the wall. Get serious, quickly. Contact Trading Standards, and if you feel a law has been broken, the police. It's as well at this stage – sad but true – to accept that your money has gone. Getting it back from someone who habitually rips off people is not impossible, but very difficult indeed. You may have to settle for a couple of other, less acceptable alternatives: making life more difficult for them, and letting the rest of the world know what they're up to.

LEGAL RAMIFICATIONS

Threatening a firm with the phrase 'I'll see you in court' may feel like a wonderfully decisive way to end your correspondence with them. In fact, it's a bit like being an *EastEnders* regular and storming out of the Queen Vic. You'll be back soon enough. What you'll find on the other side of the swing doors is that lawyers cost. No-Win No-Fee lawyers still cost, despite the name, except they'll be taking their fee out of whatever you win as costs and damages. Most won't take on your case unless there's a racing certainty to be something in it for them. If you're certain of your case, have already tried to get redress for less than £10,000 and have a stack of evidence, you could do a lot worse than try the small claims court. It's designed for cases that take less than a day, and it'll be a civil case, so you only need the balance of evidence to be in your favour (50/50) compared to a criminal court, where guilt must be proved beyond reasonable doubt (99/1). Judges are also often sympathetic to people bringing their own cases without legal representation. In practice, the other party often fails to appear, meaning that you win automatically. The downside to this is that it means they're also unlikely to pay what they owe.

Watchdog Toolkit

Looking for some support?
Here are the best places to turn:

GENERAL ADVICE

Citizens Advice
https://www.citizensadvice.org.
uk/about-us/contact-us
Consumer helpline: 0808 223 1133

BILLS

Drinking Water Inspectorate
http://www.dwi.gov.uk

The Energy Saving Trust
For impartial and independent
advice, go to: https://
energysavingtrust.org.uk/

Ofgem
https://www.ofgem.gov.uk

Ofwat
https://www.ofwat.gov.uk

CARS

Check a car's history at https://
www.gov.uk/get-vehicle-
information-from-dvla

Check a car's MOT history at
https://www.gov.uk/check-mot-
history

Get a private history check at:
https://www.autotrader.co.uk/
vehiclecheck
https://www.hpi.co.uk/
http://www.theaa.com/vehicle-
check
https://vehicle-history-check.rac.
co.uk/

The Motor Ombusman
https://www.
themotorombudsman.org/
Information line: 0345 241 3008

COMPANIES AND TRADESPEOPLE

Arboricultural Association
https://www.trees.org.uk
Telephone: 01242 522 152

Ceoemail.com
Will get you many of the direct email addresses of big bosses.

Companies House
Check a company's details at:
https://www.gov.uk/government/organisations/companies-house

Competition & Markets Authority
If you feel a contract is unfair, go to: https://www.gov.uk/government/organisations/competition-and-markets-authority/about

Gas Safe register
https://gassaferegister.co.uk

Trading Standards
https://www.gov.uk/find-local-trading-standards-office

HOUSING

To challenge an agreed rent:
www.gov.uk/courts-tribunals/first-tier-tribunal-property-chamber

Master Locksmiths Association
https://www.locksmiths.co.uk/
Telephone: 01327 262 255

The Property Ombudsman
https://www.tpos.co.uk/
Telephone: 01722 333306

The Property Redress Scheme
http://www.theprs.co.uk/
Telephone: 0333 321 9418

Removals Ombudsman
www.removalsombudsman.co.uk

Shelter
https://www.shelter.org.uk

MONEY AND FRAUD

Action Fraud
www.actionfraud.police.uk
Telephone : 0300 123 2040

Bank Safe Online
www.banksafeonline.org.uk

CardWatch
www.cardwatch.org.uk
c/o APACS
Mercury House
Triton Court
14 Finsbury Square
London EC2A 1BR

CIFAS (Credit Industry Fraud Avoidance System)
www.cifas.org.uk
6th Floor, Lynton House
7–12 Tavistock Square
London WC1H 9LT

Financial Conduct Authority
https://www.fca.org.uk/contact

Financial Ombudsman Service
www.financial-ombudsman.org.uk
Telephone: 0800 023 4567

Insurance Fraud Bureau
https://insurancefraudbureau.org
Cheatline: 0800 422 0421

Money Advice Service
https://www.moneyadviceservice.org.uk
Telephone: 0800 138 7777

The Pensions Advisory Service
https://www.pensionsadvisoryservice.org.uk
120 Holborn, London EC1N 2TD
Telephone: 0800 011 3797

Royal Mail
To report the theft or loss of post and other important documents, telephone: 08457 740 740
www.royalmail.com

Think Jessica
https://www.thinkjessica.com
advice@thinkjessica.com

NHS COMPLAINTS

Monitor
https://www.gov.uk/government/organisations/monitor
Wellington House
133-155 Waterloo Road
London SE1 8UG
Telephone: 020 3747 0000
Email: enquiries@monitor.gov.uk

PHONES AND TV

Ofcom
https://www.ofcom.org.uk

Telephone Preference Service
https://www.tpsonline.org.uk

TRAVEL

ABTA
https://www.abta.com

AITO
https://www.aito.com

ATOL
https://www.caa.co.uk/ATOL-protection

Index

ACKNOWLEDGEMENTS

Some people without whom this book wouldn't have happened. Nell Warner and Albert DePetrillo at Penguin Random House, for guiding me through the process and being patient when I was dithery or slack. Abby Watson at Ebury for letting everyone know it exists. My friend, boss and fellow *Watchdog* sentinel Rob Unsworth got this started, and routinely allows me to go right up to the cliff edge but then holds my belt so I don't fall, screaming, on to the rocks below. Every researcher, presenter, producer, director, production co-ord or manager, runner, cameraman and soundy I've ever hung out with in a studio, van or Premier Inn. You actually made it happen. Experts like Rockin' Bob and Phone Shop Charlie, Barry Cross, Mitch Westwood and James Pinder for knowing your stuff. Anne Robinson, Nicky Campbell, John Stapleton and the late great Lynn Faulds-Wood for leading the way with your brilliance, and friendship.

To my Mum and Dad who taught me what was right and what it looked like to stick up for yourself, and have watched everything – even the bits I can't watch myself.

And to my Beloved and The Wham Fam for giving me love, purpose, and the best place to come home to when it's all over.

Mx